Fear, Love, and Worship

C. FitzSimons Allison

FEAR,
LOVE,
and
WORSHIP

MOREHOUSE-BARLOW
78 DANBURY ROAD, WILTON, CT 06897

Library of Congress Cataloging-in-Publication Data

Allison, C. FitzSimons (Christopher FitzSimons), 1927-
Fear, love, and worship.

Reprint. Originally published: New York: Seabury Press, c1962.
1. Worship. 2. Fear. 3. God—Worship and love.
4. Love—Religious aspects—Christianity.   I. Title.
BV10.2.A4   1988   248.3   87-31228

ISBN 0-8192-1419-1

Printed in the United States of America
by
BSC Litho, Harrisburg, PA

ACKNOWLEDGMENTS

Grateful acknowledgment is made for permission to quote the following copyrighted material:

Author and Oxford University Press: "O wounded hands of Jesus," from Walter Russell Bowie's "Lord Christ, when first thou camest to men."

Harper and Brothers: the excerpt from Edna St. Vincent Millay's *Conversation at Midnight;* the poem "Well?" from *The Best of G. A. Studdert-Kennedy.*

Yale University Press: the excerpt from W. E. Hocking's *The Meaning of God in Human Experience;* and Walter Alexander Percy's poem "They cast their nets in Galilee."

To My Mother and Father

> from whom I have learned what I know
> of the meaning of II Timothy 1:7; and
> to whom I am inexpressibly grateful.

For God has not given us the spirit of fear;
but of power, and of love, and of sound mind.
—II Timothy 1:7

Preface

I HAVE here tried to do something quite simple: to show the relevance of worship to fear, a common problem of life. Many books have been written on the problem of fear and others on worship, but very few seek to relate the two. Most of the books on fear are psychological and most of the works on worship seem to be theological and liturgical in the academic sense of those words. This book is an attempt to place the Christian Gospel in a context of worship which is relevant to the common and universal fears of men. It seeks to be apologetic, liturgical, devotional, and evangelical at the same time. If this sounds too ambitious perhaps we should consider that the tragic mistake occurs not in combining but in separating these endeavors.

The outline of the book follows roughly that of most Eucharistic liturgies but particularly that of the Book of Common Prayer, beginning with the Collect for Purity and ending with the Blessing. However, I have tried to avoid the implication that worship is to be relegated to a service or that it is anything less than a quality of one's total life.

Much of this thought was born while I was chaplain to a conference for outgoing missionaries of the Episcopal Church. What the experience was for them I do not know, but I am deeply grateful to the members of the conference for what it meant to me.

I must add that until I tried to put this into writing, I was unaware how indebted I am to Albert Mollegen for so much of what I have to say, although he should not be held responsible for what one once called "warmed-over Molle." I am also indebted to Arthur Buckley of the Seabury Press for his skill and patience and to my wife without whom I simply could not have done this.

I pray that this book will be read "with the heart"; that it may be a fulcrum by which our life of worship overcomes, with God's love, our fear. *For God hath not given us the spirit of fear; but of power and of love, and of a sound mind.*

C. F. A.

Contents

CHAPTER ONE

Worship

SOREN KIERKEGAARD once made the observation that most of us have a mistaken notion about what a sermon is. We think of it as a play written by God, acted by a preacher, and observed by the congregation. On the contrary, he insisted, it is much more: the preacher is the playwright, the congregation is the company of actors, and God is the audience. As a congregation listens, responds, rejects or accepts what is said—remembering always that God is the witness—as they participate in the sermon, so is the sermon well done or not.

This book is about our common malady, fear; the solution, love; and worship, the means by which love destroys fear. Its effectiveness will depend, in large part, upon our taking a deep and thorough look into ourselves, our worship, and our willingness to be confronted in new ways by God. In fact, our very reading here needs to be done as an act of worship to which we give ourselves as completely as possible. We need to participate in the themes we are about to consider in the same way Kierkegaard observed we should participate in a sermon.

The Biblical portrait of Adam is a portrait of ourselves, one that has been scarcely equaled in profundity or accuracy. In Genesis 3:10 we see Adam in his disobedience, knowing that he is not what he should be and answering God's call by explaining, "And I was afraid, because I was naked; and I hid myself." This is indeed our tragedy, too. Because we are afraid, we hide ourselves from God. A lot of nonsense is talked about our looking for God and our trying to find him. Yet, actually, the reverse is the case. The classical Christian tradition from the psalmist and the calling of the Twelve to Thompson's *The Hound of Heaven* illustrates that it is not God who needs to be found, but we ourselves. Ironically we complicate the situation by hiding like Adam. Sometimes our worship is more a hiding from God than an allowing God to find us. There is a New Testament scene which helpfully describes our situation. In the parable of the talents, after the master rewarded two servants for having increased their talents, the third servant excused himself thus, "Lord, I knew thee that thou art an hard man reaping where thou has not sown and gathering where thou hast not strawed: And I was afraid, and went and hid thy talent in the earth; lo, there thou hast that is thine." (Matt. 25:24, 25) But the master took from him even what he had and said, "Cast ye the unprofitable servant into outer darkness; there shall be weeping and gnashing of teeth."

The significant point in this parable is what the third servant thought about his master. "I knew thee that thou art an hard man. . . I was afraid and went and hid thy talent in the earth . . ." The first two servants did not think their master a hard man and were not afraid; and so they did not bury their talents. Yet, in a real sense, it was not important what sort of man the master was, so long as the third servant thought him a hard man and feared him. For example, two theological students once told a friend what a hard man their bishop was. With some surprise the clergyman heard how this bishop "had razors up his sleeve," ran his diocese as if it were "a branch of General Motors," and how he "cared for statistics, not people." He was a man, they insisted, from whom you must hide your real feelings in order to defend yourself. Several months later the clergyman had an opportunity to spend an evening with this bishop and hear about the frustrations he encountered in running his diocese. The bishop complained that, before being made bishop, he had had very little trouble being a helpful pastor; but since he became the authority in the diocese, the clergy who really needed a pastor regarded him with such suspicion that he could only rarely be of real help. Conversely, the men under him who did trust him enough to have effective relationships with him were those who managed so well that they did not really need help. (It is significant that here, too, it was the servant with *one* talent who thought his master a hard man and was afraid.) The bishop went on to discuss the very theological students who considered him hard, with an understanding, affection, and compassion that were in striking contrast to what these young men thought he felt. Here again, what the bishop really felt did not matter so long as these men believed him callous and were afraid.

Our relationship with God in worship is closely tied to what we believe about him. Obviously, what was wrong with those students, and with the third servant, was that they did not believe in the love that was really there and, consequently, were afraid to the point of burying their talents. In his Nobel Prize acceptance speech William Faulkner made a similar point when he stated:

Our tragedy today is a general and universal physical fear so long sustained by now that we can even bear it. There are no longer problems of the spirit. There is only the question: When will I be blown up? Because of this, the young man or woman writing today has forgotten the problems of the human heart in conflict with itself which alone can make good writing because only that is worth writing about, worth the agony and the sweat.

He must learn them again. He must teach himself that the basest of all things is to be afraid; and, teaching himself that, forget it forever, leaving no room in his workshop for anything but the old verities and truths of the heart, the old universal truths lacking which any story is ephemeral and doomed—love and honor and pity and pride and compassion and sacrifice. Until he does so, he labors under a curse. He writes not of love but of lust, of defeats in which nobody loses anything of value, of victories without hope and worst of all, without pity or compassion. His griefs grieve on no universal bones, leaving no scars. He writes not of the heart but of the glands.

Thus, because he is afraid, the writer buries his talents and writes of only the superficial and surface things which do not touch the essence of being human because the deeper realities are buried beneath our "general and universal physical fear." It seems highly questionable that it is only, or even primarily, a physical fear of "when I will be blown up" that is the cause of our inhibited creativity, and we shall later quarrel seriously with Faulkner's solution of "forget it forever." However, he certainly seems to diagnose the cause of our common malady when he puts his finger so effectively on fear. When we are in the grip of fear we cannot think or feel deeply, nor does anything so threatened by fear seem worth the necessary agony and sweat. But is this inhibiting fear simply the fear of being blown up? Surely the fear of demons in the Middle Ages, the Black Death in the four-teenth century, utter destruction in the Thirty Years War, revolution in the nineteenth century, were all comparable to our fear of being blown up. And is it any more fearful to die by the hydrogen bomb than by the agony of the Black Death?

The fears that lead us to bury our talents and to hide from God are deeper, more subtle, and universal than merely the fear of the bomb. They are the fears of the human heart. We are afraid of being radically honest, because it will lead us to face many unpleasant matters about ourselves and our world, matters that we usually hide and cover up. We are afraid to care, because we have learned that in caring deeply we can be hurt deeply. We are afraid to be humble, because we do not think we have the strength and the courage to risk the loss of face or the blow to our precious pride that the humble life demands. Our fear of failure causes us, as par-ents, spouses, students, artists, to hedge or withdraw partially from many undertakings, even from life itself, because if we really put ourselves into an enterprise that is criticized or fails, then *we* have been criticized and *we* fail. We are afraid of being human, because being human means being free and freedom creates the hand-wringing anxieties which attend making decisions and the gnawing guilt which may accompany responsibility. We are afraid to love, because to love really means leaving the safety of our solitary lives and exposing our hearts where they can be hurt and broken and softened. Finally, we share the mutual and common fear of death that pervades, more than most of us realize, all other fears, tying them together, haunting our lives and endeavors with a threat of meaninglessness, and finally shrouding all with the dark cloud of inevitable annihilation. These are the fears that make each of us an Adam hiding from God. These are the fears that cause us to bury our lives even before we are dead. Fear itself knows only the solution of hiding and burying, but the hiding and burying is a hiding from God and a running away from our own cure.

The medicine for our "third servant malady" is the love of God: "There is no fear in love but perfect love casteth out fear." The answer to our predicament is to be found in the new Adam, Jesus Christ, for the perfect love of God is shown to us in Christ Jesus. The God of all honesty, caring, and humility, who became fully human, loved us ultimately, and failed utterly, broke through the bonds of death, thereby pouring out the power that overcomes and casts out fear. We who are afraid to be honest, to care, to be humble, to be human, to love, to fail, and to die are found and brought home by our God, who did and does and is all that we are afraid to have done, to do, and to be. This redemption liberates us from the graves in which we bury our lives and renders it no longer necessary for us to hide in fear. "For God hath not given us the spirit of fear; but of power, and of love and of a sound mind." (II Tim. 1:7)

It is all very easy to say that the perfect love of God in Christ casts out our fears and sets us free and effectively alive, but how does it do so? How does God's love give us the spirit "of power and of love and of a sound mind?" If our malady is fear and the medicine is God's love, how is this medicine applied? The answer is worship, the means whereby we are opened to the love of God.

There are, however, serious difficulties attending worship which tend to frustrate its purpose. These difficulties must be faced, not merely academically but personally, with an inquiry into the possibility of our personal misuse of worship. One of the most serious distortions which prevents worship from being effective is to act as if the whole matter is really God's problem. This is a temptation for the uninformed, casual Christian and the sophisticated scholar and mystic alike. We need continually to be reminded gently that it is not God's problem. He can take care of himself. It is our problem. It is we who are lost, half-sick, and afraid. God's love is not controlled by some heavenly cosmic valve that the angels open a little when we do something proper in worship. Everything we learn from Scripture and from Christ teaches us that the free flow of God's love is not blocked at his end but ours. *Our* hearts are hard and closed, not God's. Our worship should be directed toward removing the barriers between God's love and our fear. These barriers are nowhere but with us. It is not God who needs to be changed. In worship we are not doing something for him, except in the sense that he desires us to cease hiding and respond to his love.

A real irony is that this very activity, intended to allow the love of God to pierce through our fears in order to heal the lonely sickness of our souls, is frequently performed in such a way as to hide our real problems and true selves from God. One of the most successful ways of hiding from God in worship is to regard it as a matter of cutting out of one's weekly life a portion of time unrelated to everything else we feel, think, or are doing, and pay this to God as something owed him. Most of us only bring our real selves into worship when something has gone drastically wrong in our lives. Fishermen talk of "not having paid the preacher" when they have no luck. This is, of course, part joke, but only part. There is a vague and undefined feeling that good fortune and, in some way, heaven might be related to having been in church at least once a week. No one is sure, but then in dealing with things one cannot control such as luck and life after death, one should not risk not taking advantage of something which just might help him when he really needs it. Somehow it cannot hurt, and just to plant ourselves in a pew for an hour once a week is good "fire insurance." There is much wrong with this thinking, but the big error is the notion that worship is a ticket-punching process that gets us into heaven when we die. The benefits of worship are not for some future good fortune or something we claim to qualify us for heaven after we die. Worship is an immediate and very present means of God's love, regenerating now the fearful deadness of our existence into the more abundant life. Think what it would say about God, were it true that the meaning of worship lay in his requiring some attention from our otherwise busy lives in order to be praised. He is no neurotic third-grade teacher whose ego demands flattering, sycophantic praise from pupils. And yet, this is the inescapable implication of much of the spirit and intention of our worship. We praise God in worship with the hope in mind of some future good fortune because we have done him a favor, or that we may be taken into heaven after we die, or that we may accumulate the requisite number of good points through worship to graduate from this life into the next. There aren't any heavenly quantity credits amassed by going to church! Worship is an immediate and present means of God's love, making us new creatures and giving us the ever more abundant life *now*.

There are many factors, conscious, unconscious, and historical, that cooperate in sealing our worship from our real lives. One is the mistaken assumption that God is really interested in "holy" or "church" matters, not in those with which we are deeply concerned. Archbishop Temple once reminded us that "God is not exclusively or even primarily interested in religion." In truth, God is most interested in those very matters in which we are most involved—the feeling of estrangement from our spouse, our uncomfortableness when eating with the boss, our worries about money, and even the excitement we feel in the presence of that person who always looks so neat and whose smile is so charmingly attractive. Some of these things, however, we quite understandably seek to leave out of our worship. We would much prefer that he not interfere with the way we are now running our lives. St. Augustine spoke for us all when he said, "Save me, O Lord, but not yet." There is usually a great deal of resistance within us to opening ourselves to God in worship. The man who is planning an affair on a business trip on Tuesday is naturally reluctant to see his worship on Sunday as an offering of his total week-long life to God's love. The lady who is planning a party primarily to exclude a close acquaintance is understandably reticent to disclose her whole heart to God in worship. The "fig leaves" of our fallen nature are carried into church, too. We would like to be close to God, and be found by him, but *after* Tuesday, *after* the party.

We must also be critical of our tendency to think that worship is limited to the Sunday service we attend. To be sure, we set aside a time and place for worship, but we do so as a reminder that all times and all places can be occasions of worship. The church building is set aside as God's house to remind us that every house is God's house, but how frequently we forget this. We forget that if we confine God to a particular building for a particular hour, then we imprison him and successfully remove his presence among us. Instead, all praise and prayer, confession and absolution, hymn and sermon, the Supper and the silence, have been created to inform, influence and enlighten all praise and desires, all guilt and forgiveness, all song and learning, all meals and quiet moments of our total lives.

We are perfectly conscious of some of our attempts to hide from God. More frequently, however, we do it unconsciously. Every clergyman has had the experience of preaching a sermon especially applicable to a lady in the congregation and of being greeted by her at the door with the enthusiastic exclamation, "Oh, that was such a good sermon for my husband! I do wish he'd been here." Perhaps even our daydreaming during worship, our meal planning or replaying the last three holes in the back nine, is not so much evidence of boredom as an unconscious attempt to hide the nakedness that God seeks to clothe with his love. It is an interesting experiment to catch oneself in these distractions and ask what there might have been in the sermon or service that made it more comfortable not to hear. A couple, who were preoccupied with the conviction that the Jews were plotting to seize the country and were the dominant factor in everything that was wrong, once heard a sermon preached on the text in Philippians, "Let this mind be in you that was in Christ Jesus." The wife later said she was so bored with the sermon that she thought of how she might remake a dress to fit her daughter. The husband's reaction was equally effective in hiding himself from God. He was furious with the clergyman for meddling in political and economic affairs.

There are other effective screens behind which we may hide, like some current altercation in the parish, or our antipathy toward the minister. If we can become sufficiently furious with the preacher, his message will rarely carry for us the love of God. One lady had so persuaded herself that her minister was not Christian that every service of worship served as an occasion to gather further evidence with which to document her conviction that he was unreliable theologically. In a sense it did not really matter whether he was or not, so long as her response was, "I can't really worship God with that man in the pulpit." She had a remarkably effective smoke screen behind which to hide. And yet she is not unlike the fellow who states before the tennis game that he is using a borrowed tennis racket which is inferior to his own. He already has a built-in excuse for any failure in the game. Thousands of Christians are using the present clergyman's predecessor as a built-in excuse not to participate in the life of worship. "If only Mr. Smith were more like Mr. Jones." And the most astonishing thing of all is that even Mr. Smith will have his day when he leaves. He, too, will someday be a predecessor to someone else. Those of us who observe this sort of thing (always in others) see it only as a superficial inconsistency or an amusing eccentricity. Actually, it is a deep dodge from the touch of God and a dry journey through a spiritual desert. We do much unconsciously that hides us quite effectively from God. In our next chapter we shall go into the necessity for real honesty in worship in order to clear away the excuses, the static of hostility and bitterness, and the smoke screens of self-pity and self-justification that spoil and even vitiate our worship.

Other factors can also make for ineffective worship, factors that are neither conscious nor unconscious. They are simply the historical forms of worship which are at the same time a necessity of, yet barriers to, worship. The history of Christianity-is a story of the agonizing struggle with these forms and their misuse. A "read" prayer was seen, with a measure of justice, as a mechanical device shutting out and "grieving" the Holy Spirit. A "spontaneous" prayer as the alternative, however, was not immune to contrivance, inconsistency, and even pretension. Certainly, in the latter, the ego of the man praying was sometimes disclosed, and it hid the congregation from God as effectively as mechanical prayers. The Quakers saw that read prayers and other set forms were becoming as much barriers to, as means of, God's love. In their use of silence they recovered the power of the Holy Spirit to break through human defenses. But silence in worship is also a form, and even the Quakers must agree on the forms of time and place to worship.

Symbols are another illustration of the need for the forms of worship. The limitation of words to carry the power, meaning, and emotion sought encouraged the use of symbols which would point higher, wider, and deeper than mere words. This led to the use of vestments, objects, pictures, mosaics, and even statues in worship. As soon as any form develops, however, the misuse of it is likely to occur. For example, it is reported that in one Eastern religion a libation of milk was presented to the god in his temple. One such temple, however, was infested with mice, and a cat was kept to catch the mice. In order to prevent the cat from drinking the milk, it was tied to a pillar for the night. That was four hundred years ago, and today the service is not properly carried out unless a cať is tied to the pillar overnight. Christian worship, too, takes on forms and accessories from the past, and frequently things of secondary importance get charged with powerful emotions, totally irrelevant to their original intent, and become obstacles to the real enterprise of worship. Where should the font, the pulpit, the flowers be placed? Architecture, furnishings, vestments and all the accoutrements of worship have had far more than their appropriate emotional attention in the history of Christianity and any local parish. It is almost impossible to escape the problem of forms when even the absence of forms becomes in itself a new form. What an effective way, however, this is to avoid being confronted by God! The intensity of our feelings concerning such matters of secondary importance are often indications of our use of such things to hide from God. We are too prone to forget that all forms stand under the judgment of whether or not they communicate the Gospel; and we need always to ask ourselves how we are using them—to disguise or disclose the love of God.

Another obstacle to worship is that the Christian message itself, like the forms, has also suffered distortions. The good news of the Christian Gospel is sometimes twisted into its opposite. Worship becomes a nurture in fear rather than in love. From earliest times the New Testament portrayal of God's love has been resisted. Paul was harried by the Judaizers, who insisted, in the Pharisaical tradition, that God does not love us first and freely, but secondly, after we love him and have obeyed the law to such extent that we, in some measure, earn his love. This spirit of Pharisaism has never died out. It has pursued the Christian Gospel throughout its history and lurks in all our hearts. It is considered too good to be true that God's love is so great and free that he loves sinners and came to seek and to save that which is lost. So the Good News which should carry God's love to us who have not known the historical Jesus has become, instead of a gift from God, a prize to be won. God's love is waved as if it were a carrot in front of Christians who, if they behave, will be given a bite.

We have done this to the Gospel because we are afraid. The question has been asked for two thousand years, "If people are told that God loves sinners, what will make them behave?" The answer to this question is frequently the usual answer of any fear—one which creates more fear. "God will not love you until you are good." "God can see through buildings and into hearts. You cannot hide from him. You had better behave." Thus the love of God is cruelly distorted into a spiritual blackjack to keep people in line; it is made to appear the reward for obeying the law. Many psychiatrists and social workers have expressed deep indignation because of the lives that have been crushed by this bad news offered in the name of Christianity. Imagine a parent folding his arms and telling a small child, "Son, when you behave and cry no more, then I will love you." Yet this is the inescapable inference we must draw about the way God deals with us, from much that has been, and is being, put forth as the Christian message. And worse yet, no one has escaped completely this bad news of fear in the name of the Good News of love. A graduate student from Brazil was once assigned the task of listing the passages where the Good News was set forth in the twelve volumes of sermons by a seventeenth-century archbishop. After two weeks of searching with almost no success, he reported, "This is not the Good News, this is the bad news!"

The "bad" news has become part of the atmosphere we breathe and is an important factor in frustrating our worship. In Chapter Three we shall go further into this matter, but, at this point, we need to see that our root problem of fear is not cast out by threats of more fear. Only love can help us to break through this vicious circle that our fears have created. And therefore we must be very critical of anything in worship that makes us more afraid than we already are.

Another serious misuse of worship is to believe that we do things in order to change God's will. It is our will, not God's, that needs to be changed. Worship is not some sort of heavenly pressure we can apply to God but is a means through prayer and praise to remove the beams from our eyes to see more clearly the mercy of God. We do not sing hymns in a service to change God's mind but to open up our minds that they may be changed into that mind which was in Christ Jesus. It is simply not God's problem, it's ours. Our wills will to hide and go in the direction of destruction because we are afraid. God's will is that our wills be changed from the direction of self-destruction to the new life of love in which our wills become God's will.

The question of our wills brings us back to Faulkner's Nobel Prize speech. There he diagnoses with uncommon insight the fear that inhibits a writer's creativity and causes him to bury his talent. "He must teach himself that the basest of all things is to be afraid and having taught himself that, forget it forever, leaving no room in his workshop for anything but the age old verities and truths of the heart . . ." In other words, Faulkner tells us that our problem is fear and the solution is to "forget it forever." This sounds like nothing so much as telling a desperate alcoholic that he drinks too much. While true, it is quite unlikely to be very helpful. Would one have told a mother whose son was fighting in Korea, "Teach yourself that the basest of all things is to be afraid and forget it forever"? Do you tell a man who is chronically afraid of being inadequate to "forget it forever"? If we *are* afraid, how can we "forget it forever, leaving no room in our workshop for anything but the old verities"? This does not sound any better, nor is it any more helpful, than the common exhortation (which distorts Christianity) "to put out of your mind all thoughts of adultery" or "not to read immoral books," and so forth. Such exhortations frequently suggest the line of conduct they mean to prohibit. So, too, the exhortation not to be afraid, "forget it forever," may cause us to be even more afraid.

Mr. Faulkner to the contrary, the truth of the matter is that to change our wills and overcome our fears we need to be where our wills and fears can be touched by outside forces. Our spirit of fear needs to be where the "spirit of love, of power, and of sound mind" can be caught. An English doctor once placed an advertisement in a newspaper requesting that his three-year-old daughter be allowed to stay in the home of someone with German measles. He wanted her to contract this illness while young, so as to avoid having it later in life when it would be much more dangerous. So too, we who have the spirit of fear need to catch the spirit of love, and to do so we need to be where that spirit is. Worship, then, should be designed to make us vulnerable to the contagion of this spirit of love. There is, of course, a complex "mixedness" about our wills and our spirits. We are not totally afraid, although there is in each of us a measure of unrest and uneasiness about ourselves. In respect to almost everything important in our lives there is an ambivalence, a mixed feeling, one both positive and negative. We want both to stop and not to stop smoking; we want to be different and yet we do not want to change. We *want* to be less afraid, but not enough to *be* less afraid. This restlessness, uneasiness, and dissatisfaction with ourselves is the only qualification for worship. The struggle that a man has with himself causes his heartburn and his tragedy, but at the same time it is a symptom of his grandeur. It is the only thing in man that can be appealed to and relied upon. Man's restless dissatisfaction with himself is, at its deepest point, an indication of spiritual need and must be faced and appreciated as such. Our Lord indicates this when he said that the well have no need of a physician, but they who are sick. We cannot cure ourselves. We cannot enter into the womb to be born again. We cannot make ourselves into new people. But we can see something of our sickness and bring ourselves to a place where the physician can heal us, where he who made us can remake us, where we can be born again.

To be sure, it can be argued that all fears are not imaginary and all fear is not destructive. And with that we must agree. For there is essentially something good about being alive, and we should be afraid of failure, hurt, and destruction. The real point, however, is that our fear, even when we can justify it, does not lead us to safety but rather to hiding from that which can make us successful, whole, and alive. We need to be loved if our fear is not to bury us. Many things could hurt us and even destroy us from which our fear protects us. We protect our eyes from hurt by blinking and shutting our eyelids. However, when a cinder gets in our eye and needs to be removed it is hard to keep the lid open to remove the cinder. It is likewise difficult to open the lids of our fears in order that God's love may heal us. In any community there are many pressures that tend to make us "keep our lids closed" and thus prevent effective healing by God. A young boy training to be a church usher bungled his assignment. The head usher reprimanded him severely in front of several others. This young man learned something about worship that morning. He learned to be more afraid. He was being nurtured in fear, not in love.

Sadly enough much of the difficulty concerning worship is not the fault of the individual worshipper. We know the Christian community cannot always be trusted to heal rather than hurt. The history of Christianity is also the history of anti-Christianity. The very organism commissioned to spread the spirit "of power, and of love and of a sound mind" has too frequently enhanced, fed, and encouraged the spirit of fear. This is especially true of worship. That enterprise in which we need most the freedom to hear, feel, and have communicated to us the love of God has often been twisted into a most complicated social and liturgical obstacle course with many hazards.

Obviously, the most important factor in worship is the community that does it. A community can distort the whole meaning of Christianity by being cold and unfriendly, and thereby causing such loneliness and rejection that words of love cannot be heard. On the other hand, a community can be so relaxed that the individual can safely let down his defenses and be vulnerable to the spirit that casts out his fear. The real irony of our lives, however, is that the very mechanisms and mannerisms, the reactions and responses, that we have developed over the years to defend us from hurt are at the same time our defenses against love.

In effectual worship it does not matter what our natural abilities are, nor how profound the sermon, nor how exquisite the music, if the gathered community does not allow us to relax, if it does not make us feel it unnecessary to be afraid. To kneel together to confess our common sins, to be bound together in the common relief of absolution, to share our mutual praise, fear, concerns, and frustrations, can provide us with a measure of the security necessary to open ourselves to the goodness and love and joy that pours from God through honest worship. John Wesley has been criticized for the rigor with which he weeded out back-sliders from among the newly converted. But Wesley was keenly aware that anyone so opened to the love of God after a life of fear was also vulnerable to new fears. These newly-touched Christians needed to be surrounded by a community that showed love and not fear, especially when their defenses had been penetrated and torn down and a measure of God's love had warmed their hearts. We are warned in Scripture about having a demon cast out and seven more entering in.

Because the defenses against love are the same defenses as those against hurt, any worship that breaks down these defenses must be seen as a serious and possibly dangerous enterprise. What makes the difference between a dangerous experience involving our vulnerability and a saving experience of God's love reaching deeply into, and re-creating, us is the quality of our community. Even when alone, we are still a person in a community. Our feelings and fears are largely determined by our relationships. We cannot, therefore, ever worship alone in the sense of our ever really being cut off even in memory from others. Worship then must be seen as a corporate, mutual, and interdependent enterprise.

A terrible judgment must always hang over the Church.

Is it a community that is feeding fear or nurturing love? Judgment also stands over the individual as a part of the community, forcing him to ask continually what sort of spirit he is contributing to the community, whether he is helping or hurting. A very likely exegesis of that passage in Matthew 16:19 concerning the keys of the kingdom is that in fact the Church is binding and loosing in everything it does. Obviously it is no mechanical key. The opening of men's hearts to the love of God so that the kingdom of heaven may be within them is something the Church does in the entire life of worship. It is also true that church communities can nurture the fear that binds the heart from God's love and his kingdom. In every activity in which it engages, the worshipping community ought always to ask itself whether it is binding or loosing, hurting or helping, enhancing the need to fear or communicating the love of Christ.

To be sure, fear is not a completely bad thing. In fact, fear, and the anxiety that accompanies it, are signs of life itself. Only the dead are neither anxious nor afraid. Fear is like pain. Pain is unpleasant and destructive, but if it were not for pain we would be in danger of dying before we knew we were sick. As pain is therefore a guardian of health, so fear has a similar relationship to love. Pain can be seen as an anguished cry for health. Fear is likewise the sign and signal of our need for God's love. John Donne expresses it well: "The Love of God begins in fear, and the fear of God ends in love; and that love can never end, for God is love."

It is not enough to see that the solution to man's predicament is the love of God in Christ. We must also see our personal fears behind which we hide from God. Participation in such an inquiry can help open our lives in an effective worship that will allow God to find, heal, and love us. Nothing quite as simple and external as a bomb can be blamed for all our fears. We need to examine the deeper fears of our hearts and perceive how these specific and personal fears are overcome by God's love in worship. We shall consider what seem to be the universal and common fears of the soul and see how these are overcome and cast out in a recovery of the true worship that opens us to God's love. We shall have an opportunity to face squarely the deepest fears that cause us to bury our talents and hide from God and see how our worship may become the means by which God can make us the new people he intends us to be.

CHAPTER TWO

The Fear of Being Honest

EFFECTIVE worship demands honesty, and without it we cannot expect God's love to be administered or our fears to be overcome. Adam, we recall, hid himself because he was afraid, and the third servant buried his talents in the earth for a like reason. We, too, hide ourselves from God, bury our talents by becoming deeply and subtly dishonest, and clothe our fears with the fig leaves of fantasy and self-justification. True worship, however, requires us to face real situations, not rationalizations. Adam blamed his disobedience on Eve: "She gave me of the tree." Eve blamed the serpent: "The serpent beguiled me, and I did eat." Ever since, man has looked outside himself for a scapegoat or an excuse. An insurance adjuster once estimated that 90% of people involved in automobile accidents see themselves as blameless. The reason we distort our real situation, clothe it in excuses and illusions, is that we are afraid. Worship cannot help us, cannot be the means whereby God's love casts out fear, unless it is honest. Thus we face a dilemma: our fears make us dishonest, but only honest worship can be efficacious. How then can we begin to worship with the appropriate honesty? The answer is that we can take only one step at a time. The first step is to realize that none of us is completely honest in all our worship, and the second, to begin our worship with a sincere intention to allow the experience to bring us closer and deeper into those areas that we have unknowingly covered up and hidden from God's love.

At the outset of our quest we are frequently all too willing to have medicine applied on a symptomatic level rather than on the deeper level of the real causes of our common spiritual sickness. A man once went to a doctor desiring a salve to cure his rash. The doctor saw that the real cause was an inadequate diet, but the patient refused to allow the doctor to change his customary diet. Instead, he insisted upon the medicine alone, and very little actual healing resulted. Neither the doctor nor the medicine was at fault. The doctor's hands were tied as long as the real malady was not confronted. Similarly, in our worship, the areas we are willing to open to the medicine of God's love are those which we find most comfortable to admit and disclose, but we strenuously resist opening the unpleasant areas which are the real basis of our fears. Yet the areas we are least inclined to face, the situations we are most "touchy" about, are the very ones that need to be touched by God's love. It is always much easier and less unpleasant to admit that we do not go to church often enough or that we smoke too much, than it is to face honestly the fact that we do not really love anyone, not even ourselves, let alone God, with all our heart and mind and strength. However, if we are sincere about our worship, an honest beginning is essential. Indeed, it can even be said that the efficacy of our worship is dependent upon our honesty. There must be no hypocrisy. We cannot base our worship on unreal conditions and then complain that the real conditions remain untouched.

This is all very easy to say, but much more difficult to grapple with. The business of being really honest in all things is difficult and painful, more so than we usually realize. A friend who, with the help of a psychiatrist, was trying to learn the true source of his difficulties described this long drawn-out experience as one in which "he was walking around all day in water up to his waist." The sheer emotional energy expended in the search made his daily normal routine exhausting. Any clergyman will testify that his most difficult pastoral problems are those in which the person is convinced that the cause of his difficulty lies in his external situation, in his office or in his home. What he is really asking of the minister is to support this appraisal, and he will resist considering the possibility that his own spirit may be responsible, in large part, for the unfortunate external situation. The man "whose wife doesn't understand him" usually finds it painfully unpleasant to acknowledge his share in the responsibility for the inadequate mutual understanding. A very wise pastor once described us all as being stuck together with the glue of the illusions which we have about ourselves. To have these illusions taken away is to become "all unglued." Indeed, honesty is not only difficult; it has its dangers, too.

Ibsen's *The Wild Duck* is a dramatic example of the danger of honesty. After several years' absence from home Gregors Werle, the young man in the play possessed by the "claim of the ideal," returns and shows his father that he, the father, was responsible for much of the tragedy in the life of Gregors' mother. Possessed by the "claim of the idea of absolute honesty," Gregors shatters all the carefully constructed illusions of his acquaintances. In fact, no illusion by which an individual lives and cushions the hard blows of life escapes Gregors' merciless pursuit. The local physician says that Gregors himself is sick, and he diagnoses the malady as "an acute case of integrity."

There is a young girl in the play, who lives in a sad, barren house with old people, but whose life is brightened by a crippled duck which she has healed and tamed. Around this pet she has constructed a beautiful and happy world of imagination. She participates vicariously in the duck's freedom of flight and delights in the wonderful vistas of mountains and sea, fjord and snow, sunsets and rainbow, which it sees. All this is in stark contrast to the dark and somber life she leads amidst the tragic lives around her. Gregors perceives the role of the duck as an escape from the harsh reality of her earthbound existence and insists, in the name of honesty and reality, that this illusion be destroyed. He persuades her to take a pistol, climb to the attic where the wild duck is kept, and destroy this fantasy forever.

She takes the pistol and goes to the attic. For a moment there is silence, then Gregors hears the shot ring out. He smiles, satisfied that one more dishonest illusion has been stripped from the real world. But when the silence continues, he goes to the attic himself and finds that she has not shot the duck but has turned the pistol on herself. This "acute case of integrity" thus culminates in the suicide of a fourteen-year-old girl.

Only very callous people can be unaware that for many people life is worth while only because of their illusions and fantasies. It is only bearable because of their excuses and self-justification. But it is not merely exceedingly arduous to be scrupulously honest, it is actually dangerous. There is a sturdy basis for our fear of being honest. Overcoming this fear is not a casual part of the life of worship. Indeed, the first step is to realize its presence.

Ibsen, in his anatomy of honesty, has been called the father of contemporary drama. Whatever the defects of modern drama mǎy be, the plays of William Inge, Tennessee Williams, Arthur Miller, and Eugene O'Neill do show, with agonizing unpleasantness, the profoundly tragic difficulty of being honest. Usually the opening of one of these plays shows the common scenes of life. Then, little by little, as these ordinary people confront each other, painful tensions and conflicts come to light. The agony in modern drama is almost invariably provided by the character's gradual self-realization, which develops as his or her illusions are destroyed.

Because self-realization means agony, we all are prone to resist such scrupulous honesty. Our case is not unlike that of the four-year-old boy with a splinter in his foot, who cries from the pain it causes but is afraid to have his father remove it.

Adults have many splinters in their hearts. Bitterness and resentment, envy and hatred, are covered up, only to fester and become infected, beneath illusions of self-righteousness and self-pity. Unlike physical splinters, hatred and bitterness can become so much a part of us that they acquire a sickening sweetness which we use to flavor all our dealings. A man was once fired because he reported a colleague for unethical behavior, not knowing that the colleague was the nephew of his boss. That was thirty years ago; but this man continues to trace, in some way, each subsequent inadequacy to this injustice. Recently he was injured in an automobile accident; and, of course, this would not have happened had he been working for the original firm rather than traveling for the present one. Needless to say, any attempt to remove this splinter of bitterness, which has become so useful in self-justification, is met with hostile resistance. Many of us come to worship, not to be healed but to have the whole fabric of our self-justifications and illusions fed, nurtured, and strengthened.

Or take the suppositious case of the active church member whom we shall call Mrs. Villiers. She rarely misses a church service, sits in the front pew, and gives generously to the church. However, there exists in her life a terrible tragedy—her husband is an alcoholic. When her children were growing up, she attempted to insulate them from the unwholesome influence of their father. But the younger son has not succeeded in business despite the very generous assistance she has given him. She complains, not very convincingly, that the older son has not married and that her married daughter with two children only rarely comes to see her or asks her to visit. If it were not for the church, Mrs. Villiers claims she would be unable to exist. Her alcoholic husband and two ungrateful children she sees as the cross she must bear, and the strength to bear it she gets from her life of worship.

Her reaction to these misfortunes is revealed in her biblical question: "Didn't God choose the most righteous Job upon whom to send suffering?" It could well be, however, that this is not so much Christian patience as self-pity seeking support. These misfortunes may not be so much the cross of Christ she must bear, as splinters caused in part and sustained by self-righteousness.

Suppose a Gregors Werle were her minister, and he were to explain to her the responsibility she must share for her family situation. "Look, Mrs. Villiers, it is in part at least because of your domineering desire to run the lives of your children that one is unmarried, another irresponsible, and the third ungrateful. You must face the real situation. You are not the innocent victim of misfortune. You are an aggressive and possessive person who has violated the self-respect of your husband and prevented any independence on the part of your children save by their rebellion." Like Gregors Werle, this clergyman would do more harm than good. But what can he do? Does he smile when her worship becomes the scaffold for the structure of her self-justification? Real life is always more involved and complicated than this theoretical illustration. It is very hard to live with an alcoholic and have children who are ungrateful; and few people can stand an honest unqualified confrontation with themselves and their situation. This leaves us with the sober fact that false worship, which nurtures illusions of self-justification and self-pity, prevents the love of God from casting out fear; while true worship which requires a measure of honesty is not only arduously unpleasant, but can be dangerous as well.

Even our prayers sometimes have a threatening import. One very alarming prayer, dating from at least the ninth century, points out that none of our clever disguises hides the naked truth from God.

Almighty God, unto whom all hearts are open, all desires known, and from whom no secrets are hid; Cleanse the thoughts of our hearts by the inspiration of thy Holy Spirit, that we may perfectly love thee, and worthily magnify thy holy Name; through Christ our Lord.

All of us are glad that the girls in the bridge club or the boys at the office do not know all about us—about that time in the Navy when . . . or after the high school dance when . . . or when we lost our temper and beat one of the children in a way we cringe to remember. Without a doubt we are relieved that only our spouse knows about some of these things. Then, of course, we are further relieved that even our spouse does not know of other things in our hearts and our desires. In addition to the things we have done, there are the things we have not done, the opportunities missed because of our callousness and insensitivity. The depth psychologists tell us that the worst, the most painful, and the "awfullest" aspects of our inner life we hide even from ourselves. And yet honesty requires us to face all our desires and feelings, confront ourselves as the persons we really are. How can we stay in church when we pray such a prayer?

The simplest way is to miss the prayer by being late. A more complicated way is gradually to persuade ourselves that our righteousness not only exceeds that of others in church, but is of such quality that it is God who should be grateful. However, this requires a continual process of self-justification on every occasion of blame and responsibility. Simple inattention, or a combination of inattention and spiritual rationalization, will also do quite well. However, if we are to take seriously this prayer and face the reality that God knows, why do we not get up and hurry out of his house? ". . . unto whom all hearts are open, all desires known, and from whom no secrets are hid . . ." Of course, the answer is that God knows *and* God loves. But we must not be too facile with this answer. We must see ourselves and our problem in depth before this answer of love can be mediated through worship to us.

The Law, which represents God's demands and his will, helps to reveal the true sources of our difficulties. A young man who has made no graven images, whose parents are dead, and who has neither committed adultery nor murdered during the week might, of a Sunday, tick off quite casually the Ten Commandments. But he cannot meet the demands of the Summary of the Law with the same confident assurance: "Thou shalt love the Lord thy God with all thy heart . . . and thy neighbor as thyself." Sometimes we think we love God with all our heart, but what about our love of neighbor? Are we not really like the people who say, "The more I see of people, the more I love God." We are really fooling ourselves if we believe we love God, when we have no compassion for our neighbors. The Bible calls us liars. "If a man say he loves God and hateth his neighbor he is a liar."

No worship is effective unless we allow the Law to probe behind our illusions or lies, into the hidden areas which desperately need the love of God. St. Paul described the Law as the schoolmaster who leads us to Christ. In leading us to Christ, the Law must deal severely with these symptoms of our sickness, cutting through them to the real causes. The situation at the office, those socialists, my spouse, the payments on the car—all these are smoke screens hiding the real sources of our problem. We must allow the Law to cut beneath these superficial matters, remembering that we worship not for approval of things as we see them but in order to receive the diagnostic judgment of the living Word. The pile of unanswered mail on the desk, the unpaid bills, the uncomfortable experience of identifying oneself with the elder brother in the parable of the Prodigal Son, are all judgments of the Law that can become the very occasion and beginning of a new life of love because they press us toward the real situation which needs attention. In the life of worship every demand upon us, every law and obligation, can become a means of breaking away from the vicious circle of fear—the fear that breeds dishonesty, the dishonesty that hides the source of fear.

The Law, when used as a diagnostic instrument of love, leads us out of our fearful fantasies into the reality of God's love. Of course, a surgeon's scalpel can be a very destructive instrument depending upon who uses it and how. So law, demands, and obligations can be very destructive elements in our life. To be creative, then, the Law must be seen in the context of the Gospel. The varied and continuous demands upon our lives need to be seen as coming ultimately from the love of God. The good news of the Gospel, that God not only knows but cares, enables us to open ourselves where God's love is most needed. Inasmuch as we hear the Gospel, we are enabled to breach the opaque prison walls of our intimate hypocrisy, bitterness, resentment, and self-pity. We hear this news not only with our ears but in our hearts, and not only through words but through the actions of people. It was in the person of Jesus Christ that this news was made known. All the real and horrible danger of being honest was realized on the cross, where Christ cradled the honest truth in the context of love, love unto the very end. Thus, hearing the Gospel through the non-threatening defenseless love of God in Christ can evoke from us an ever-deepening honesty.

Honesty grows with faith. When we come to know God's love, we are able to see, in the Law and in the demands of life and reality, something of the will of God which is directing us towards health and love. A young salesman, convinced that his inability to sell his company's product was caused by the inefficient, unpleasant sales manager, was afraid of the tenuous status of his job. One day he was astonished to overhear a telephone conversation in which the manager indicated that he was pleased with the young man. Although he still thought the office could be managed better, the young salesman realized, for the first time, that that was not the real reason for his poor sales record. Previously he could not bear to look at the sales chart posted each week. Now he saw the chart as a helpful reminder of the real situation and looked at it with a positive spirit even before his sales showed a marked increase. His ability to be honest and effective was helped by the "law of the chart," but only after he had heard the good news of his status. Similarly, as long as we have not heard the Good News of our status with God, we can only regard the Law of his demands as irrelevant and destructive. Thus, we need to be reminded continually of God's love in order to manifest the honesty necessary for effective worship.

We need *to hear* in order to be honest. We need to hear again that "while we were *yet* in our sins Christ died." We need to hear and understand more deeply the story of the woman taken in adultery, of the prodigal son, of the lost sheep, and of the lost coin. Pascal pointed out that "Jesus Christ is a God whom we approach without pride, before whom we humble ourselves without despair." In order to begin without pride, with a non-despairing humility, we need to hear anew, in its profundity, the basic theme of the Good News as set forth in the epistles to the Galatians, Romans, and Ephesians. We are, indeed, sinners—but we have been justified by Christ. The combination of all our good deeds, plus all our clever excuses and self-justifications, is not adequate to deserve God's love—but it *need not be.*

The case of Stypulkowski, the Polish underground fighter who became a prisoner of war in Russia, illustrates this honest hearing we are talking about. This man was one of sixteen Polish resistance fighters who had bravely struggled from 1939 to 1944, were taken prisoners, and tried before a Russian court for war crimes. Prior to the trial the office of the Prosecutor put these men under a rigorous period of interrogation in order to be able to elicit from them at the trial the confessions the Court wanted. The method pursued was that of placing the prisoners, during the interrogations, under such pressure as to break them spiritually and destroy their integrity, thus leaving them quite open to suggestion and influence and ultimately ready to make the craven confessions the Court desired. Of the group Stypulkowski alone did not break and faced the Court with his plea, "Not guilty." And this despite the fact that on 69 out of 70 nights he had been brutally interrogated in a series of 141 interrogations. Not only did he endure these incessant interrogations, but in the process he broke his first interrogator who had to be replaced. If we can understand something of how Stypulkowski withstood this ordeal, we shall be able to see how the tensions in our lives can also be overcome.

Courage can be weakened by guilt. Hamlet pointed to this in his remark, ". . . and conscience doth make cowards of us all." Everything that Stypulkowski did, or did not do, was examined for its guilt content. For example, he was questioned in something of the following fashion: Should he have worked for the aims he did? If so, why did he not work harder? (In such a serious business as working in the underground a slothful slip or a lapse in judgment could endanger men's lives.) Did he not feel responsible for many deaths? (The conflict in loyalties is always a fertile ground for guilt.) Did Stypulkowski not endanger his family, who had been imprisoned, by his attitude of resistance for the sake of Poland? Had he always been really faithful to his wife, family, country, and God? At one point when Tichonov, the first interrogator, was exploring the question of Stypulkowski's ambition, he twisted the matter around, urging Stypulkowski to give in and thus serve Poland better. Here the aims of the prisoner were used to encourage compromise and thus weaken his integrity.

Any of these exploratory areas could have become avenues to guilt; and when discovered, stripped of excuses, and exacerbated, they could bring about such remorse and despair as to sever the very nerve of courage, even threaten the elementary instinct of self-preservation. Ironically, too, the more conscientious the individual, the more distressing he would find the questions.

After weeks of almost nothing to eat, sleeplessness to the point of exhaustion, the calculated terror of the prison environment, and the incessant interrogations designed to break and destroy his spirit, Stypulkowski was confronted with what was the most insidious of all temptations. He was shown the distorted confessions of his fellow prisoners implicating him. First it was only hinted, then spelled out quite plainly, that a plea of guilty would certainly lessen his sentence, whereas a plea of not guilty would doubtless result in a much more serious sentence, probably death. In other words, he was offered his life for the price of a small compromise. If he succumbed, his inner integrity would be gravely wounded by his choice of life over honor and honesty. This would have been the beginning of his downfall. If he succumbed, his jailers would know his weakness and this could be further used until all self-respect was gone and he was broken indeed. But not to confess would mean that he would die, never seeing his family or country again. Perhaps worse, he would rot in some unknown prison deep in Russia. Yet Stypulkowski refused to confess to something he did not do or to being what he was not. He even went on to plead not guilty at the trial.

The most impressive part of Stypulkowski's account of his imprisonment is the unselfconscious but quite natural mention he makes of his faith. His Christian faith was kept alive, in this ordeal, by regular prayer; and all loyalties to self, family, and country were obviously subordinated to his loyalty to God. It is quite clear from his account that Stypulkowski knew that he was not without weaknesses. He knew, in fact, what they were, and when they were pointed out to him, he was never surprised. The interrogator could, in effect, say to him: "You are known as a brave man; but you and I know that you were terrified at every threat of danger. You are known as a religious man, but you are not even wholesome because you are defiled with lewd thoughts and dirty deeds. You are not brave; you are a coward. You are not honest; you are a hypocrite." This kind of thing— this showing a man his own image with all its weaknesses, cracks, and flaws can be a shattering experience.

Stypulkowski, however, was not shattered. And the reason is clear. In his worship he had continually presented himself to God as he actually was, had been accepted, and had been forgiven. He was beyond being taken by surprise by his own weakness, inadequacy, and guilt. Having been forgiven sins much more serious before God than the charges made by his interrogators, he could refuse to admit false guilt to an earthly tribunal. He did not rely on his own righteousness. He could later, quite humbly, say: "I have never felt it necessary to justify myself with excuses. When they showed me that I was a coward, I already knew it. When they shook their finger at me with accusations that I had filthy thoughts and lewd feelings, I already knew that. When they showed me a reflection of myself with all my inadequacies, I could tell them, 'But, gentlemen, I'm much worse than that.' You see I have been taught since I can remember that it was unnecessary for me to justify myself. One has already done this for me, Jesus Christ.' " This strength was unassailable. As St. Paul declared, "Who is he that condemneth? It is Christ that died."

Life itself is not unlike an interrogator. In less dramatic ways, but sometimes equally desperate ones, we are stretched on the rack between honesty and self-respect, and our excuses and the demands of life. The simple unselfconscious faith of Stypulkowski can be an example of how the life of worship gives us the power of honesty, "for God hath not given us the spirit of fear but of *power* and of love and of a sound mind."

It is a grave mistake for Christians to overlook the arduousness and danger involved in being honest, but it is equally wrong to assume that being honest is a miserable, terrifying enterprise. On the contrary, when real splinters are pulled, real healing begins. Reality is never as bad as the fear of it. Ibsen, O'Neill, and the modern dramatists rarely show the relief and reconciliation which can occur when the illusions and lies are taken away. The Christian believes in the essential goodness of reality and creation. The real difficulty is not with the world or with God, but with our fear and the forms it takes. In facing squarely the real painfulness of truth, we can also see the power and joy that comes in the clean humble worship of Christ whom we approach without despair.

CHAPTER THREE

The Fear of Caring

LIFE quickly teaches us that caring causes hurt, and so the most easily understood of all fears is, perhaps, the fear of caring. Each of us has only to consider the occasions of hurt to realize that it was our caring that made us vulnerable. Perhaps one occasion was someone's death. We read every day of people being killed, but since we do not know or deeply care about them, we feel no pain. When someone dies whom we know and love, however, we are hurt quite poignantly. In fact, our hurt, it would seem, is in direct proportion to our caring. In this chapter we must consider how and why we are afraid to care, and how worship may become the means of the love that casts out this fear.

One evening a young man came home, looking very dejected, and when asked about his dejection, he replied, "I won't have anything more to do with girls." He had cared, had been "kicked," and was consequently hurt. His response was more than merely adolescent. He had discovered the universal relationship between caring and hurt. Hence, to avoid future hurt he would not put himself in the vulnerable position of caring. Some years ago there was an expression going the rounds of young people: "I couldn't care less." When a young person was most concerned, but realizing his vulnerable state, wanted to hedge and withdraw, he attempted to persuade himself and others that he really didn't care at all.

The hard fact that must be faced is that Christian caring is in no way immune to the hurt that accompanies any other caring. The hurt, if anything, is deeper because the caring is deeper. St. Paul's life was relatively safe while he was a Pharisee. As a Christian, however, he was beaten, persecuted, thrown into prison, and finally martyred. He tells us himself of the perils, pains, and suffering of his Christian vocation. In addition to these adversities, his Christianity led him to care for others to the point where he exclaims, "Who is weak, and I am not weak? who is offended and I burn not?" (II Cor. 11:29) His own vulnerability is widened to encompass the cares and hurts of all. Being hurt is the radical threat involved in being Christian. There is no cheap way out, no bargain-counter Easter. The symbol of Christianity is not an overstuffed chair, nor a paid-up pension plan for retirement from life, nor a safe bank vault, but a cross.

Our Lord called his disciples with a simple invitation. He did not ask them to memorize the Creed, the Lord's Prayer, or the Ten Commandments. He simply called them to follow him. They must have known something of this man— that he was one who cared deeply; and they also knew, no less than we, that to care is to be hurt. This man, Jesus, went around defenseless, caring with an open heart. It was he, the one who cared, whom they were invited to follow. "Follow me" is the invitation to Christianity—the invitation now as it was then. Acceptance of this invitation is faith. Faith is much more the courage to care than it is belief in doctrine. Jesus did not ask his disciples to shout assent to the creed. He asked them, and he asks us, to respond to his love with the courage to care, to follow him.

The disciples who responded to this invitation began to care—and to know hurt. Their lives are aptly described in the hymn by William Alexander Percy:

> They cast their nets in Galilee
> Just off the hills of brown;
> Such happy, simple fisherfolk,
> Before the Lord came down.
>
> Contented, peaceful fishermen,
> Before they ever knew
> The peace of God that filled their hearts
> Brimful, and broke them too.
>
> Young John who trimmed the flapping sail,
> Homeless, in Patmos died.
> Peter, who hauled the teeming net,
> Headdown was crucified.
>
> The peace of God, it is no peace,
> But strife closed in the sod.
> Yet, brothers, pray for but one thing—
> The marvelous peace of God.

An understandable temptation is to distort this scriptural understanding of faith, the *"care-full"* response to God's love and its vulnerable consequences of hurt. The most common distortion of it is to make doctrine, creed, and dogma into "the Faith." Doctrine and creeds are more important than many appreciate because they are expressions, directions, and descriptions of what the faithful believed. They are consequently very important as means of bringing us to the object of faith, our Lord Christ. But the creed itself is obviously not the object of our faith.

The history of Christianity indicates two major errors in failing to make a proper distinction between faith and doctrine. The first is making faith into an intellectual assent to doctrine. This is quite understandable because it involves none of the New Testament risk of caring. It is obviously safer to say "yes" to the creed than to respond to God's love in caring as he and his disciples did.

The other mistake is believing that we can respond properly to God's invitation in faith without aid and direction from teaching and doctrine. We were not there fishing with Peter and John, and we can only respond as we know who it is that is calling us. We know that Jesus was not a phantom, as some actually insisted in the second century (Docetists), because we have been taught the doctrine of those who had known him. Those who have had the courage to care by responding in faith to Christ know him as fully man and fully God. Their teaching can lead us to Christ as guides and directions. It is sometimes helpful to think of doctrine as a map. It shows the way to go and is drawn by those who have been there. It would be folly and a bit arrogant to ignore this help and set out alone. If one were going to New York from Los Angeles, it is possible to set out without consulting a map or sign board; but it would be imprudent to ignore the directions built upon the experience of those who had been there. It would be equally absurd to fill one's study with a library of maps in place of going there. Some of us avoid the invitation of Christ to follow him, by fill-ing our shelves with books on doctrine and by believing that faith is assent to the creeds which embody correct doctrine. Others are never confronted with the Christ and his invitation because, being ignorant of Christian teaching about him, they do not know who he is.

Our worship cannot be effective unless we respond in faith. This faith is neither doctrine nor belief in doctrine, but courage to care, courage to do the very thing we are afraid to do. In St. Mark's Gospel little children are brought to Jesus and the disciples rebuked those who brought them. Jesus said to them, "Suffer the little children to come unto me, and forbid them not: for of such is the kingdom of God. Verily I say unto you, Whosoever shall not receive the kingdom of God as a little child, he shall not enter therein." (Mark 10:14-15) It is obvious from this scene that some childlike quality is necessary in the Christian response to God. One of the things that happens as we grow up is that we become increasingly afraid to care. Hence, much of the pressure of life as we grow older causes us to lose that childlike willingness to care.

Arthur Miller shows us something of the pressures of life that cause us to lose these childlike qualities. In Miller's play *Death of a Salesman,* Uncle Ben tells Willy Loman in front of his sons, "Life is a jungle, Willy; be hard. Some go into the jungle and find the diamonds. Others get caught by the tigers. Life is a jungle, Willy; be hard." This pressure in life to be hard is not confined to being a salesman. Doctors and nurses feel the pressure, particularly when surrounded by so much suffering and tragedy. If a clergyman should care more, he would perceive even more tragedy than he now finds weighing his heart with a breaking load. It takes a real measure of toughness as a parent to watch one's own child suffer the inevitable pangs of life without dominating that life. There is no place to hide, no occupation to enter, where the pressure of being hard does not threaten our simple childlike willingness to care. Because of our fear of being hurt we grow cautious and lose the warmth and spontaneity of children.

Mary Chase has shown us a man who, even as an adult, has retained this childlike warmth and spontaneity. Elwood Dowd, in the play *Harvey*, is a remarkably attractive character. He can walk into a bar, sit down with his drink in a booth, and people flock to him as nails to a magnet. They see in his face some quality of fresh awareness and sense in his countenance real compassion. They come over, sit down, and tell him of all the big bad things they have done and the great good things they are going to do. Then Elwood introduces them to Harvey. Harvey, who sits next to Elwood, is a seven-foot-tall rabbit whom no one else can see. In these times one doesn't talk with imaginary rabbits without eventually talking with a psychiatrist. So Elwood is taken to a psychiatrist who tells him, "If you'll begin by taking a co-operative attitude, that's half the battle. We all have to face reality, Dowd—sooner or later!" To this Elwood replies, "I wrestled with reality for forty years, doctor, and I am happy to state that I finally won out over it. My mother used to say to me, 'In this world, Elwood, you must be oh, oh so smart,' or 'oh, so pleasant.' For years I was smart. I recommend pleasant. You may quote me."

Underneath the charm of this popular comedy is a distressing theme. It would appear that the only way we can retain our childlike caring and warmth is with two crutches. As adults, either we become hard or we limp through life with our true humanity propped up on one side by the crutch of alcoholic stupor and on the other by that of an hallucination of a seven-foot rabbit.

How can we retain this childlike quality amid all the pressures of life without an alcoholic stupor or a retreat from the pressures of reality? How can we as parents, doctors, salesmen, and politicians be both soft and tough, be at the same time warmly compassionate and efficiently capable? Another way to ask this same question is: how can we have the courage to respond to, and have within us, God's spirit "of power, and of love, and of a sound mind"? Much of our worship is designed to answer this very question. Once we see that the faith required in worship is primarily our willingness to care in response to the invitation of Christ, then we are beginning to communicate with God. As we have seen, hearing the Gospel enables us to be honest. So also being forgiven reveals to us a quality of God's love that penetrates our fears and nurtures our courage to care.

Confession and forgiveness are integral and continual elements in the life of worship. In facing and confessing our sins we continue to build upon the firm basis of honesty that undergirds all truly Christian worship. We know that God knows. The problem is not what we can hide from him but what we can face that he already knows. As we face, admit, and confess our sins, we experience the forgiveness that carries the courage to care. One reason for the joy in heaven over a sinner's repentance is the unique power which comes with forgiveness. The repentant sinner, having been forgiven and having been taken back like the Prodigal Son, learns a lesson of love that the righteous do not know. On his return the Prodigal knows the power of the father's love much better than he did before he left. This curious and alarming spiritual fact, that a forgiven sinner has experienced a measure of God's love he did not know before he sinned, has upset many people, especially those charged with the responsibility of morals. From the very beginning this fact led some to ask St. Paul, "Then should we sin that grace may abound?" Of course not, but the alarming quality of this part of the Gospel has led the principle of forgiveness to be denied and the consequent power lost. Still the Pharisee, in all ages and perhaps in all hearts, sides with the elder brother and warns that this news of free forgiveness is not a sufficient guard against sin. The difficulty with the Pharisee is that he lays burdens on us without first giving us the necessary strength to bear them. Christ's burden is light and his yoke easy only when we ourselves are carried by his forgiveness.

A sergeant told a grim joke to his trainees during the Second World War, which shows the real flaw in the Pharisaic understanding of Christianity. A man stopped on a dirt road to help get another man's car out of the ditch. The latter was beginning to harness two small furry kittens to the bumper of this huge car when he was asked, "Mister, you aren't going to try to get those kittens to pull that car out of the ditch, are you?" His reply was, "Why not? I've got a whip." The lash of the Law is used in similar spiritual situations. Without the principle of forgiveness our conscience acquires a quality of cruelty that makes the Gospel of Christ anything but the Good News.

It is perfectly incredible how the unmistakably clear and simple fact of God's forgiveness of sinners has been so frequently denied throughout the history of Christianity. There is a story of a clergyman who had an argument with a vestryman about whether a woman of bad reputation should be made welcome in the church. Finally the minister said,

"Well, didn't our Lord forgive the woman taken in adultery?" "Yes," replied the old gentleman, "but I don't think any more of him for having done it." The humor in this should not hide the serious fact that the Gospel has been and is being distorted and each of us can assume that much of the power of forgiveness has yet to be applied through our life of worship to our fear.

In fact, the tendency to deny the New Testament principle of forgiveness began with the second generation Christians. Referring to Christianity of the second century, Bishop Kenneth Kirk states that writer after writer seems to have little other interest than to express the genius of Christianity wholly in terms of law and obedience, reward and punishment. Adolph Harnack states, "When the Apostolic Fathers reflect upon faith, which however happens only incidentally, they mean a holding for true of a sum of holy traditions, and obedience to them, along with the hope that their consoling contents will yet be freely revealed." Thus, early in its history Christianity was in large measure cut off from the power and grace that comes from forgiveness. Tertullian, in the third century, insisted that Christianity provided for only one sin after baptism. This view was so prevalent that it was common practice to delay one's baptism until the end of life in order not to use up this radically limited forgiveness. Recovering the principle of forgiveness at the Reformation was a great contribution indeed, but it was only too soon obscured by a new Protestant scholasticism.

Luther's followers tended to equate faith with intellectual assent to creedal statements instead of wholehearted commitment of the entire man, which Luther himself had rediscovered in the New Testament. The recovery of this principle of forgiveness is the most significant factor in the vital movement begun by John Wesley. However, the resistance is always so great that every age needs to discover anew the experience and power of God's free forgiveness which is continually available to us all. We can generally assume, regardless of our tradition, that we have not been adequately "let in on" this part of the Good News.

St. John tells us quite plainly, "If we say we have no sin, we deceive ourselves and the truth is not in us. If we confess our sins, he is faithful and just to forgive us our sins and cleanse us from all unrighteousness." Our repentance and God's forgiveness is an experience that enables us to care. We need not "sin that grace may abound." We *are* sinners and need only to confess that grace may abound. When we are forgiven and taken back as the Prodigal was, this experience gives us assurance of love that we did not have before. This assurance and new-found security gives us new power or grace. This grace then gives us courage to care, the faith with which we respond to God's love in the new life of caring.

Before we can be forgiven, however, we must face our sin, confess, and repent. We must continue that honesty which is necessary for all true worship. We must worship "in spirit and in truth." The honesty that undergirds all true worship will bring any man to his knees. We must realize that the sin we confess is not merely something we have done but perhaps something we have felt: bitterness, lust, resentment, self-pity, ingratitude, or hatred. The sin we must confess is not merely that we are thoughtless and do not love our spouse or neighbor or colleague as we should, but that we are in a situation of being separated from the very ground of our being, from God. We are in this situation, called sin, because we will to do our will rather than the will of God.

And usually we turn to God only when we have come to some "dead end" in our lives, some tragedy, frustration, or suffering.

The great thing about facing our separation is that forgiveness is always available even in these "dead end" times and in the pig-pen experiences of our prodigal nature. Another great fact is that spiritual energy, released in experiences of forgiveness, is enormous. Guilt, conscious and unconscious, when bottled up, unforgiven and unresolved, saps and draws away our vitality physically as well as spiritually. One of the primary causes of despondency is unresolved guilt. As Adam was afraid of God because of his guilt of disobedience, we are afraid in part because of our feelings of guilt. When our guilt is unresolved and our fear becomes chronic we become unhealthy physically as well as spiritually. As we have seen in the first chapter, fear in itself is not always a bad thing. When we are afraid our hearts pump unusually fast to provide the blood necessary for extra power to our tensed muscles. This complicated physical reaction to fear was very desirable when the object of our fear was a tiger in the forest. It enabled us to cope more readily with such dangers. However, in a civilized situation with its more subtle objects of fear the physical reaction to chronic fear can become a terrible drain on our bodies and cause much of our fatigue, insomnia, or listlessness.

Procrastination, due to not feeling energetic enough to accomplish what needs to be done now, can be the result of having much of our energy already dissipated in struggles with chronic fear arising from unresolved guilt. A mother who is guilty about her impatience with her children can become possessed by the consequent fear of being an inadequate mother. This chronic fear stemming from guilt over her impatience can waste so much of her physical energy that she has little left for picking up toys and attending to the needs of the family. Confessing impatience and being forgiven can cast out her fear and set free energy and power she did not know she had.

Another unfortunate result of guilt is that if unforgiven, it seeks to resolve itself in destructive ways. Lives can thus be seriously impaired. A college sophomore confided to her chaplain that she intended to run off and be secretly married the next week end. She had spent the night with her date and felt a secret marriage was the only way she could make amends. She believed it would be hypocritical to be dressed in white and married in church. The disappointment in not having the kind of wedding she had always expected would in some way perhaps atone for her wrong doing. The negative reaction of their families would also serve to punish her as she felt she deserved. Here is a good example of how guilt when unforgiven naturally seeks to resolve itself in self-punishment which is often quite destructive and unhelpful. She began to understand that the planned secret marriage would only be another mistake that would not rectify the previous one. It would be neither fair to their families nor to their marriage. She saw that in part this decision was arrived at because of the disappointment it would involve. We frequently deal with guilt by punishing ourselves, hoping in a distorted way to atone for sin by our suffering.

This same chaplain is convinced that many students in college do not pass because of their "need to fail." In fact, he argues persuasively that many failures in the general endeavors of life are results in part of the "need to fail," caused by feelings of guilt. This guilt, neither confessed nor forgiven, lives like a parasite by feeding on the life of the host. It would be impossible to estimate the energy and creativity sapped and dissipated by guilt, but it is certainly prodigious. A wife can feel that an unhappy marriage is a just propitiation for previous wrong doings and thus be inhibited in any attempt to improve the marriage. In spite of what she *thinks,* what she *feels* is important. She may know intellectually that it does not help the past to suffer unnecessarily in the present; but if she feels guilty, she will be tempted to seek and endure unpleasant situations. One wife who could not bring herself to protest her husband's rather open infidelity was probably inhibited by guilt of her own past indiscretions for which she felt unforgiven. She was irrational in her inability to protest this present threat to her whole family. Thus, guilt untouched by forgiveness resolves itself in an infinite variety of destructive ways causing unnecessary suffering and anguish and apathy. The same dynamics which cause people to think that "the more they hate and punish themselves, the more God will love and reward" cause us all to allow our guilt to cripple our lives. The experience of repentance and forgiveness can overcome this self-sabotage, the distorted "need to fail."

Every experience that demonstrates God's love to us helps us to increase our ability to care. God's love is most clearly seen in his forgiveness. As we repent and are forgiven, our ability to respond to him is strengthened. The relationship between fear and faith is shown frequently in scripture. "Why are ye fearful, O ye of little faith?", Jesus asks his disciples. Our faith, our response to God, our courage to care is increased by God's forgiveness. Our fears are overcome when we are taken back and made to know that we are his. Jesus frequently used the example of a family to describe the qualities of the kingdom of God. A child's relationship to his family is one that is ideally so constituted that he is unmistakably shown by the parents that no matter what happens he belongs to this family. Security evokes honest facing of our negative situations. A child's transgressions are dealt with severely, yet in a context of his acceptance as a part of the family. Such correction can be a clear indication of love because it shows that the parent cares enough for him to be bothered to discipline. Many children seem to "ask for it" as a test of their parents' love because it takes real love to discipline firmly and creatively. As the child is cared for, he is enabled to care in return.

So in our worship, as we face our own unworthiness and experience God's love in forgiveness, we are enabled to respond by caring. Faith itself is a gift. This courage to care is not something we can decide to have. We cannot even decide to believe. We can only decide to act in trust. We cannot make ourselves care when we simply do not care. We are given the courage to care by being cared for in the forgiveness of our sins. Our God who first loved us breaks through our fears to care, with the terrible cost of the cross, and in penetrating our wall of fear gives us the power to care.

In worship we try to set up a situation that will allow God to reach us through our fears. One reason why stories about little children seem to evoke much more emotional response than similar stories about adults is perhaps that children, being relatively helpless, do not threaten us as adults do. Hence, a story of a child slips past defenses of fear to that warm, soft place in our hearts where we can still care. We will allow ourselves to care for a child who is less likely to hurt us than an adult. Once several adults sat in a parlor waiting for a funeral to begin. Everyone was exceedingly uncomfortable until a small child came in with her mother. Almost immediately everyone was put at ease by the presence of this unselfconscious child who evoked quite natural and relaxed attention from the adults.

Our Lord comes as a child on Christmas and slips by our fear defenses in a way that perhaps an adult could not do. However, as Jesus grows up he retains that childlike vulnerability. He carries no sword. He weeps on learning of the death of Lazarus. He is easily hurt. He is nailed to a cross in a most vulnerable position with not even one arm available to protect himself. No one has explained fully the exact meaning of Christ's suffering for our "at-one-ment" with God, but at least in part it is a concession to our fear. "He came not to condemn the world but that the world through him might be saved." The opening words of the angels to the shepherds were, "Fear not for behold I bring you good tidings of great joy . . ." We need to see the baselessness of our chronic fear. We certainly have no fear of this man pinned to a cross with nails in his hands and feet and spear wound in his side. To penetrate our fear to care, God became vulnerable to evoke the faith that receives love and casts out fear.

It remains that in accepting his invitation to follow him, we do get hurt. Caring costs, and the caring which costs the Cross will indeed break our hearts, too. Yet that is what our hearts need. As we become more afraid to care, our hearts grow harder and we become less alive. The Christian Church is the society of the brokenhearted. "The sacrifices of God are a humble spirit, a broken and contrite heart thou wilt not despise."

Bishop Lancelot Andrewes in a sermon prepared to be preached on Easter Day, 1624, deals with the phrase from Hebrews 13:21, "make you perfect in all good works." He suggests that the verb, *katartisai,* translated "make you perfect," means "to set you in joint." "That our nature is not right in joint is so evident that the very heathen . . . have confessed it. And by a fall things come out of joint, and indeed so they did . . ." Good works are not possible, Andrewes states, until we are "put in joint." Since the fall in Adam our hearts have been "out of joint." Our fear to care causes our hearts to need resetting, to be "put back in joint." We are broken anew to heal and grow straight.

Even though true Christian faith causes our hearts to be broken by the hurt that comes with caring, it is now no longer lonely. There is little that is more deadly than loneliness. Our fear to care leads us inevitably toward loneliness, leaving us alone from people, history, creation, and from God. We need to hear in new ways this indispensable element of the Gospel, the forgiveness that nurtures our ability to care and overcome our loneliness.

Dr. Reuel Howe tells a story that is a vivid illustration of the principle of forgiveness. The mother of a spoiled young child, an attractive but harassed housewife, was beginning to realize that love demands a real firmness. She refused a request by the child to do something quite unreasonable but the little girl whined and cried and finally threw herself on the floor in a real tantrum. The mother with great internal distress stood firm. The child finally gave up in exhaustion and went upstairs to her mother's bedroom. She pulled her mother's best dress from a hanger in the closet, took pinking shears from the sewing maching drawer, and began to hack the dress to pieces. Her mother, "hearing the silence" as perhaps only mothers can do, came upstairs into the bedroom where her daughter sat crosslegged on the floor with the dress in her lap irreparably cut to pieces. In despair the mother threw herself on the bed sobbing. "Mommy,

Mommy!" the little girl said. But her mother failed to hear over her own sobs. Again the child said, "Mommy, Mommy!" Hearing this time she raised her head from the pillow and asked, "What do you want of me now?" "Just take me back, Mommy, just take me back."

The most important factor is not the precise discipline given the child but that it be done in the context of the daughter having been taken back. Is anyone callous enough to miss this all-important principle in the relationship between parent and child? "If ye then, being evil, know how to give good gifts unto your children, how much more shall your father who is in heaven give good things to them that ask him?" (Mark 7:11) If we are taken back by our parents, and as parents have this kind of home in which children are undergirded with a love that is not bought or earned but given, then how much more so is the love of our father in heaven?

Confession and forgiveness in worship are the means by which God nurtures our courage to care and feeds our faith in opening ourselves to his love. This experience of forgiveness occurs in formal services of worship and informal gatherings over coffee and tea. All occasions in which we are fully known and accepted and in which our shortcomings are forgiven are experiences that strengthen our courage to care for a better world in history, for all men including our enemies and those closest to us, for ourselves, and for our God who first cared for us. All our caring for creation, the future, our neighbors, and ourselves is ultimately dependent upon our care for our God. Thus, our confession and forgiveness in a service of worship stands for and includes the Christian nature of all confession and forgiveness in our whole life of worship.

CHAPTER FOUR

The Fear of Being Humble

SOME OF the reasons we fear to be humble are well illustrated by Bridget Boland's play *The Prisoner* (later a movie, starring Alec Guinness and Jack Hawkins). The plot is based upon the story of a Cardinal in an Iron Curtain country who has been taken prisoner by the Communist police, made to confess to outrageous crimes, and thus removed as the leader standing in the way of a completely integrated Communist state. The Cardinal, in this instance, is an unusually capable, self-sufficient, strong personality who has already withstood extreme torture at the hands of the Nazis. As we have seen in the Stypulkowski story, the Communists break a man's spirit by breaking him spiritually. The police interrogator first studies his subject carefully to find the weaknesses which can be used to destroy his integrity. A man's armour is seen as "chain mail, a clattering skin of linked weaknesses, all holes just twisted together." When the weaknesses are discovered and the subject is faced with them, there arises an overwhelming need to unburden in confession these deep and subtle feelings of worthlessness. But he is refused the opportunity of making a straightforward confession until his need to confess is so great that he will use any form of confession, even subscribe to crude and untrue charges which can be popularly exploited by the Communist press.

The first chink in the Cardinal's armour appears when his relationship to his mother is probed. A coffin is brought in and he is told to open it. He does so and finds the body of his mother. The Cardinal assumes she is dead, but when he kneels to bless her, he touches her forehead and finds it warm. He rises and demands an explanation. He is told that unless he signs the confession, she will die a very horrible death in a cancer hospital. The Cardinal, faced with this dilemma, paces up and down and finally wheels, shakes his finger in the face of the interrogator, and says that he will not sign the confession and that his mother's death will not be his fault. The interrogator here breaks into a cynical and triumphant smile. He has discovered the weak link. Not only does the Cardinal not really love his mother, but he is apparently more concerned with the status of his own soul ("it won't be my fault") than with the life of his mother. "If she must, your mother can die of pain—to save your immortal soul. You are a hard man, Eminence, a hard man."

There was some grain of truth in this charge. As a very sensitive young boy the Cardinal had been deeply offended by his mother's immorality and could remember men visiting her at night. He was driven by a determined desire to get as far away as possible from the smell of fish associated with the area of their early home and from all uncleanness.

Since his rise in the Church's hierarchy he had provided in material ways for his mother, but he felt neither compassion nor warmth toward her. In fact, the probing of the interrogator began to show that he felt very little genuine love or compassion for people generally. Oh, he was scrupulously honest, an indefatigable worker, an efficient administrator, and an excellent preacher. He never went into the pulpit without painstaking preparation, and he could always draw upon his thorough educational background; but his sermons were not motivated by a poignant concern for the fears and hurts of the people in the congregation. On discovering this the interrogator asks him how he was able to look into the people's faces and eyes. The Cardinal replies that he had learned very early to look at "the spaces between their heads" when he preached.

Gradually, the Cardinal is brought to see how unloving he actually has been beneath the exterior of his ecclesiastical and popular success. He begins to be convinced that even the good things he has done were motivated by pride and self-centeredness. Even his courageous stand before the Nazis and his brave behavior under the Communists were based more on his desire to justify himself than on any grateful response to God. His sermons were well done, not because of an overflowing love for people hungry for the bread of life, but because his self-respect would not allow mediocrity in anything. In subtle and complicated ways the Cardinal is led to the conviction that everything he has ever done, even the best things of which he is most proud, are tainted with the self-centered motives of pride. Allowed very little sleep and subject to constant interrogations, he reaches the point where he can no longer stand the growing, gnawing conviction of his own guilt.

It is not enough, however, merely to confess. He has to make restitution. He is brought to the conviction that his religious vocation has been only a role he unconsciously played to rise above the squalor of his origin and to justify himself before men. As the interrogator puts it, "Yes, you've lived a good life, haven't you? For the greater glory of you, for the making of a Prince of the Church, for the proving and perfecting of the miserable little bastard of a backstreet drab who smelt of fish." Under these conditions the Cardinal was convinced that he had stolen the honor of the people and that it must be given back. Permission is granted to confess, but the Cardinal is led to see that he must also make restitution for the honors which had been heaped upon him and which he now knows he did not deserve. He wants to confess that his whole life has been "a fantasy to hide me," that he became a "priest for my own glory and that all my service was to my own spiritual pride." But here the interrogator points out that this confession will not make restitution for his undeserved honor, stolen from the people. He must confess in such a way that the people will understand. A confession made in the way he is proposing, argues the interrogator, would be interpreted as saintly humility, and he would be canonized in twenty-five years. To make restitution he must confess in terms that will give up all claim to the honor in which the people have held him. Thus he is led to believe, for a period of twenty-four hours, that it is absolutely necessary for him to state publicly that he has been a bad priest, that his whole life has been a lie, that he has stolen money from the church, that he has betrayed the people of the resistance, and that since the war he has been a real enemy to the people. This he does to a shocked court and to the dismay of the free world in order to make restitution for the acclaim and respect his pride does not deserve.

He did "break" and he did fail to withstand the Communist pressures. But something else happened, too. The interrogator, who was being congratulated on his success, had been thoroughly disturbed by his confrontation with the Cardinal. The prisoner, to be sure, was "broken," but in the process the interrogator had witnessed a courage he had never before known. The Cardinal's willingness to face any and all possibilities about himself, no matter how disagreeable, without lying or twisting the reality with face-saving versions, manifested a courage heretofore unknown to the interrogator and indicated a source of power unexplained and unknown in Communism. After the trial the interrogator points out to the prisoner the weak point in his armour. "You believed me when I told you your whole life was built on pride. A proud man would have been more sceptical." Yes, he had broken the Cardinal, not only through his pride which all men have but through his humility also. But at the same time the humble willingness of the Cardinal to believe his own unworthiness had disclosed a source of strength and human grandeur the interrogator had not known. "God hath chosen the weak things of the world to confound the things which are mighty." (I Cor. 1:28)

Shaken, and with a sad determination to rectify in some way what he had done to this man whose depth of courageous humility only he knew so well, the interrogator goes to the cell and reveals that instead of being executed the Cardinal will be released to face the crowd of people who now believe him to be a traitor. This is a much more terrible sentence than death. The Cardinal had faced and accepted the fact of his execution, but this is a new and deeper trial. Having discovered something inexplicably wonderful in the strange combination of weakness and strength, of pride and humility, the interrogator offers to shoot the Cardinal and thereby avoid the more cruel and unusual punishment of being turned free to face a disillusioned and hostile public. The prisoner declines this escape, and when asked how he has managed to make peace with himself in the face of people who will judge him, he replies, "He who will judge us is he who made us." This calm confidence manifested a quality of peace that even the interrogator perceived. "So you've found here a peace you never really knew outside. Perhaps you should find it in your heart to thank me." The Cardinal answers, "The doctor who diagnosed the weakness? Perhaps I should." Even the most diabolical tragedy becomes an occasion of diagnosis handed over in worship to the Physician of our souls!

At this point the most significant thing in the play occurs (which was somehow omitted from the motion picture). The Cardinal asks about his mother. He is told that she is alive and well. "Thank God!" he exclaims. Reverting to the "old interrogator," the Communist sneers, "For her sake, or yours?" Very quietly the Cardinal replies, "For hers. I have more sympathy than I had with human weakness." Out of the brokenness of tragedy is here born the spirit of compassion.

The Cardinal leaves the cell and walks into the crowd of strangely silent and uncomprehending people. He walks with a courage that comes of the knowledge that he is ultimately immune to any but God's judgment. He walks with confident silence in marked contrast to the proud Prince of the Church whom we saw at the beginning of the action. He walks powerfully, with that incongruous, slightly slow-footed gait, his head neither down in shame nor up in arrogance. He walks with something certainly not far removed from the peace of God.*

The puzzling irony is that the honesty which led the Cardinal to follow the destructive and diabolical plan of the interrogator was also that which made such overwhelming effect upon the interrogator. His defeat and failure seemed to produce a capacity for compassion ("I have more sympathy than I had with human weakness") and for the peace of God. Here we can see something of the meaning of the cross and resurrection of Good Friday and Easter. Here is an example of impeccable integrity and unusual efficiency, based in large part on pride, broken in a horrifying tragedy of defeat and failure, but rising again in victory. Perhaps this victory can be perceived only with the eyes of faith, but it carries with it qualities of peace and, most of all, of compassion that were not there before.

There is a very subtle relationship between pride and humility which *The Prisoner* can help us understand. This chapter is about our fear to be humble and how this fear is overcome in worship. We are afraid to be humble because of the implicit threat to our pride. There are few words which are as confusing as "pride." It would seem that it is the basis of everything noble and yet we are told that it is the root of all sin. Even in the dictionary it can be seen as a synonym both of "self-respect" and of "arrogance." Dickens, when condemning pride, said he did not mean that sentiment

---

* Alec Guinness, who played the part of the Cardinal in the movie, was not a Christian, but the power and profundity of the play so impressed him that his experience of playing the part led him into the Christian life, and he joined the Roman Catholic Church in the middle of filming the movie. The irony is that this film, one of the best pieces of Christian literature written by a Roman Catholic and one which made such a profound impression upon Alec Guinness, is banned in Ireland and Italy as being anti-clerical!

a mother has for a child, because that was not so much pride as a combination of two Christian virtues, faith and hope. Scarcely a congregation has not been puzzled and a bit upset when pride was condemned from the pulpit with quotations from St. Augustine or Reinhold Niebuhr to the effect that pride is the root of all sins. We all know that without pride the family, the school, the company, and the individual would lose most of what is worth while in each. How then is this almost indispensable factor the root of all sin? There are several cheap ways to escape this dilemma. One is the semantic method. We merely say that *false pride* is wrong, arrogant, and the cause of sin; whereas true pride is the noble spirit of self-confidence. But this does not tell us how to distinguish between true and false pride, and it fails to show that both good and bad do indeed flow from the same source.

What the theologian means when he says that pride is the root of all sin is that when analyzed carefully, any sin can be seen as the result of our self-centered desire to be the center of the world. We may recoil in disbelief when we are told that pride is the desire to be God, because few of us have any awareness of a desire to dethrone God. However, when we tell a lie, we are in fact attempting to describe reality and creation in a way that is more conducive to our desires. One lie usually makes it necessary to tell another, and the second a third, and so on, until in principle a lie represents our desire to create a world in which reality is more in accord with our wills than God's will. The same is true of murder. Our wills come in conflict with the will of another. We cannot actually create a retroactive world which does not contain this object of our frustration, but by shooting him with a pistol we can create a world in which he no longer exists. It is also true of envy and adultery. We may covet another man's wife, wishing that God's world were one where she is ours. We may try to create this reality by breaking God's law, thereby attempting to set our lust as the law of this world in opposition to God's world in which she is not ours to desire or have. Any sin, then, in this profound sense, is an attempt to usurp God's will. The serpent tempts Eve with the suggestion that "ye shall be as gods." This is indeed our difficulty from the time when as children we failed to share our toys until adulthood when we begin to cheat on our income tax return.

Yet this drive in us to do our own will does accomplish some very wonderful things. How many hospitals have been built, books written, industries developed, and even United Fund drives fulfilled because of man's desire for acclaim, respect, honor, and reward? In fact, who would shave or bother to keep the house swept if it were not for pride? The reluctance on the part of any congregation to ascribe all sins to pride is understandable. Pride is the source of many of the good things in life. Our reluctance to accept humility as a substitute for our pride is also understandable. Would people not take advantage of us? Wouldn't we be losing the major force in our very lives? Yes, people will take advantage of us, and, yes, we shall lose much of the motive power that keeps us half-way decent citizens.

Yet, it is not without real cause that we are afraid to be humble. True humility requires us to give up that which is, for the most part, the very basis of our life. Few people have reached the point of having their entire life based upon the kingdom of God. Albert Camus' novel *The Fall* was acclaimed by some reviewers as the profoundest understanding of sin since St. Augustine. Though not a Christian, Camus showed in this work that everything Jean Baptiste, the protagonist, did was merely a subtle expression of pride. Here was a famous and respected lawyer who defended the indigent without fee, who was apparently kind and unselfish in all that he did, who even had begun to agree with the many people who considered him unselfish and humble. That is, until one night he stood aside and made no effort to save a young woman who threw herself into the Seine. In analyzing his apparently uncharacteristic behavior, Jean Baptiste came to see that one powerful factor in his failure to act was that he had had no audience. Then he began to see that his whole life had been one of role-playing. This terrible revelation forced him to re-examine all his other acts that had been applauded and respected. He began to discover that when he peeled away their outer husks, these "good deeds" were merely subtly disguised forms of a malignant egoism. All his life he had craved to be respected and have people in debt to him for his many kindnesses. He even remembered tipping his hat to a blind man he had helped across the street as if he were bowing to an audience. The more he analyzed, the deeper the levels of motive he probed, the more egocentric all he had ever done or was became starkly clear. The recognition of his true self cut him to the very quick so that he no longer had the vitality to carry on his popular and respected life. This case history of Jean Baptiste is a good example of the anatomy of pride and the dangerous possibility that, in diagnosing and exposing pride as the motivating center of one's being, we can lose the source of much of our vitality. Hence, it is more than a mere misunderstanding of terms when people resist the disclosure of pride as the root sin. It is a firm and justified feeling that in rooting out pride they will be giving up much that is worth while in life. What will remain when this pride is taken away? Few of us may be aware how deeply entrenched within us is our fear to be humble. Yet it is a very powerful reality in our lives.

Even the figure in *The Fall* at the very bottom of his stripped-down life has yet one treasure of self he does not release. Somehow Jean Baptiste knows that the rotten self-centeredness he has discovered in himself is also present in all others, even if they are not aware of it. He has one final superiority—a deeper insight into his own sin. "However, I have a superiority in that I know it and this gives me a right to speak." In other words, he can feel he is more humble than anyone. It is rather like the man who talks of writing a book to be entitled *Humility and How I Achieved It*. Or like the case of the three friends who gave blood to the Red Cross: each was given a stick pin showing a drop of blood to wear on his lapel; two of them did, but the third kept his in his pocket and was warmed by the knowledge of his greater "humility." Illustrations such as these can be rehearsed endlessly, and they point to the bottomlessness of man's pride and the self-defeating tencency of his endeavors to be humble. Indeed, a Franciscan has even been reported to have given credit to the Benedictines for creativity, the Dominicans for scholarship, the Jesuits for discipline, only to claim the simple virtue of humility for his own order.

These cases are all rather humorous, but they are also indicative of the deep-seated universal nature of the problem. Somehow the problem cannot be attacked directly. We cannot seek humility itself, without developing a more subtle form of pride. St. Augustine once exclaimed, "O man, what is thy malady?" He answered his own question with the one word, "Pride." The solution to the problem certainly does not lie merely in an intellectual understanding of it. No one ever considered himself more well-versed in understanding this matter than a certain professor in a theological school. He knew the problem and saw the answer in God's action on the cross. He knew that Pharisaism is the best example of religion based on pride, because the Pharisees trust in their own self-righteousness. He considered it a primary duty of a Christian today to struggle with the new Pharisaism as St. Paul had with the old. To illustrate his point he tells this story: He had once been involved in a rather unpleasant discussion concerning the true meaning of the Christian Gospel. Later an old friend came to see him, and he related to his friend something of the discussion. At each point the friend agreed with the professor's position. Finally, the friend observed, "There is one question that when squarely faced diagnoses all Pharisaism: Who crucified Christ?" The professor immediately nodded his head in vehement assent and exclaimed, "That's right! The damn Pharisees did it!" The friend made no comment. He knew that he had inadvertently trapped the professor in a response which really expressed a new Pharisaism. For the only Christian answer to the question propounded is, "I crucified him." Any other answer is Pharisaism.

The self-righteousness of pride, in the words of Jeremy Taylor, "dies divisibly and fights perpetually, and disputes with hopes of victory, and may also prevail." All self-righteousness is judged on the cross, and to be a Christian is to see one's own self-righteousness as that which makes Good Friday necessary. If it were merely the Romans or the Jews or the Pharisees who made it necessary for our Lord to die, then it is not we who were forgiven on the cross, and we are yet in our sins. If we do not feel the guilt of God's suffering, then we cannot feel the forgiveness of his having done this for us. We must still base our reliance upon our own righteousness and thus be new Pharisees ourselves. The quotation above from St. Augustine was not all that he had to say. "O man, what is thy malady? Pride. And the remedy? Behold the humble Lord!" Here then is where we must begin to see how worship may be the means of overcoming our fear of being humble.

We are rarely exhorted in scripture to be humble, because the Christian religion comprehends the tricky quicksand present in the relationship of pride to humility. Humility is a fruit of the Christian life. We cannot become humble simply by giving up our pride. Humility is not something we can seize. To approach it directly with the intention of attaining humility will only lead one into more subtle avenues of pride. It is a by-product of leading a Christian life. People regarded as saints in the history of Christianity are a diverse and dissimilar lot, but they seem to have one thing in common, something of that humility we see in Christ. And yet none seemed self-conscious or aware of being humble. They did not seek to be humble but to follow the humble Lord.

This is done in the life of worship, not just in a service but in an entire life that does continually "behold the humble Lord." How then is the fear of being humble overcome in worship? There is an important rule of thumb in worship: *we become like that which we worship.* This can in part be understood when we notice how people tend to copy or unconsciously mimic those whom they respect. In one law school there was a widely respected visiting lecturer who, when he spoke, had a habit of grasping his lapels and rocking upon the balls of his feet. It is said that a whole generation of lawyers adopted this practice of grasping their coat lapels and rocking back and forth as they addressed the court. Who has not observed how young boys at summer camp will pick up the mannerisms of some respected counsellor? One high school teacher insists that his students walk with a decided swagger on Wednesday mornings after watching the Wyatt Earp show on television the night before. If it is true that we tend to copy or emulate that which we respect, it is much more so that we tend to become like that which we worship. Of course, this is in part what the Incarnation is all about. As St. Athanasius pointed out in the fourth century, "He became as we are in order that we might become as he is." We see in Christ not only what God is like but what we are to be is our intention and destiny. Our worship, our life of beholding the humble Lord, is the means whereby we may become as he is.

Thus we see the importance of what we worship. There is nothing in creation that man should worship because every created thing is less than man in his intention and destiny. That is why Moses was angry with the Israelites when they worshipped the golden calf or some other idol. Jewish and Christian worship always pointed man above himself and creation toward the source of that image in which he was originally made. Though some people may deny the divinity of Christ, most admit that it is an essential part of the Christian belief. However, many do not know, much less believe, (and it is infrequently emphasized in the history of Christian thought) that Christ is fully human, even as we are, as well as divine. To ignore the humanity of our Lord is to miss half the Gospel. We can see what our humanity is really meant to be in Jesus Christ. The Christian's norm is not the statistical average of some ethical or religious Gallup poll but the perfect humanity seen in Christ Jesus. Here in the life of Christ is the measure by which we see ourselves. This is why Christianity is at the same time the most pessimistic and optimistic of all religions; pessimistic because of the sad and tragic discrepancy between what we are and what Christ is, and optimistic because our destiny is more glorious than anything of which we have dreamed.

The solution lies in becoming, on conscious and unconscious levels, like the humble Lord whom we behold in our worship—who became as we are in order that we may become as he is. We are not asked to be humble in any abstract sense. There is a certain frustrating impossibility about any abstract decision to substitute humility for our pride. Instead, we need first to live the Christ life, and then humility will be an unconscious fruit. Humility will be a description of our life when it is brought before the Cross.

A non-Christian humanist once made the point to his Christian friend that a modern French novel contained a profound religious observation. It seemed that there was an island inhabited by naked penguins who were living quite innocently and happily until a missionary came and told them they were naked. The penguins set about making clothes, but one small attractive penguin made her tuxedo skirt a trifle short. Another penguin observing this fact knocked her on the head and dragged her into a cave. The upshot was that her brothers killed him and his brothers began seeking revenge until the whole colony was full of sin and warfare.* Before the Christian could answer, the man's own wife turned on him with the sharp and unanswerable observation, "John Mills, if you think you can get back into the Garden of Eden simply by taking off the fig leaves, you're crazy!"

What is wrong with us cannot be cured by putting on fig

* This is obviously not an accurate recollection of Anatole France's *Penguin Island*.

leaves or by taking them off. What is wrong is that we need to be transformed and re-created. The fall of man was seen by Athanasius as analogous to a picture that had been torn and whose image had blurred. Suppose a fine oil painting of yourself which hung over the fireplace had fallen in your absence and been punctured by an andiron. The heat of the fire caused the paint to run, blurring your features until your image was scarcely recognizable. Who is it that can restore the original image? Only the original creator himself. The doctrine of original sin is nothing more than the teaching that we are fallen from the state of original righteousness, that we are not now in our present image what we were designed to be originally, or will be ultimately. Few people who deny the truth of original sin realize they are denying such a positive and glorious belief in our intention and destiny. To deny the doctrine of original sin is in effect to accept the distorted image that each of us represents all there is to man's glory.

Christianity teaches that each of us, in his inmost self, is another Adam who, through pride, can destroy himself in a bewildering, fascinating, and infinite variety of tragedies. It is as though our pride were a broken power-steering mechanism that tended continually to pull us off the path of our true destiny. Ironically, we cannot be repaired by taking away our power to steer—namely, our freedom—because it is part of our humanity. That kind of repair would be like the "successful" operation which incidentally killed the patient. The repair to our fallen image must be accomplished without destroying the very precious and delicate force of our humanity. Many, many sure cures for man's physical illnesses cannot be used because the cure that eradicates the particular disease happens also to eradicate life itself. Likewise, spiritual cures for man's state will cure but also kill. One can give up pride and freedom by eradicating both. If it is true that pride and freedom cause our sin, we can eradicate our pride in a kind of spiritual suicide and give up our freedom to a priest or a dictator (along with anxiety, responsibility, and guilt that go with freedom) and thereby cure our sin. And, of course, one can cure hiccoughs by sticking his head in a bucket of water three times and pulling it out twice. We can commit spiritual suicide by some cures for pride.

The cure that we are offered is the cure of the new Adam, Jesus Christ, who came to re-create our fallen image. It is of the utmost importance to realize how careful Jesus was and is not to destroy our pride and freedom. He refuses to give a sign that would so overwhelm the senses that our response would be coerced. There is always the possibility of our rejection of him, then and now. The real cure can only come in a form that will not destroy our nature but will heal and re-create it. This makes it necessary for love that transforms our pride to work through our freedom. Hence, we are simply asked to behold the humble God. This means that we take ourselves and our immediate situations, frustrations, conflicts, joys, gratitudes, and place them before the Cross in continual acts of worship. Our pride that leads us into activity but then causes our jealousy and resentment is brought before the humble Lord. We put ourselves where help can be applied to our malady.

This is precisely what the Cardinal did. Imagine how hollow and meaningless an exhortation to humility would have been for the Cardinal as we saw him at the beginning of the play. He took his pride into the situation life presented him. He faced the matter with a remarkable measure of honesty, and it brought him to apparent defeat and destruction. In this tragic dilemma and painful experience he found something more solid and secure, more creative and powerful, more peaceful than his pride upon which to rely. The inner man now possessed a buoyancy in faith that gave the strength for compassion which pride could not give. In this example, as in all life, these matters are ones of degree. The Cardinal, of course, had some compassion and faith before this experience, but he had much more afterwards.

There are, however, many tragedies without victory and many sufferings without new creations. What was it that made the Cardinal's defeat into victory? What was it that transformed his pride from arrogance to humility with its peace and compassion? First of all, he was honest. He did not hide from God with excuses for his egoism but faced it and admitted it. Second, he showed that he had heard in a real measure the Good News that Christ, by whom he was made, would be his judge. Thus, he who understood him and loved him while he was yet in his sins was the only judge who would ultimately matter. This judge had said, "Come unto me all ye that travail and are heavy laden and I will give you rest." This he did. The Cardinal brought his burden of guilt before the humble Lord who forgave him.

It is significant to compare the figure of the Cardinal with that of Jean Baptiste in *The Fall*. Both experienced the agony of realized egocentricity, the discovery of the subtle power of pride in their lives. However, the results are strikingly different. Jean Baptiste gave up the good in his past life and spent his time in bars telling of his fall. The Cardinal, on the other hand, returned to his previous activities with qualities of his true humanity he had not before possessed.

It is worth while to reread and carefully study Camus' *The Fall*. Some critics claimed that it heralded Camus' imminent conversion to Christianity. The lawyer Jean Baptiste does indeed seem to pierce through the illusions of self-righteousness that clothe our pride in a most prophetic way. And what is his name? Is it merely an accident that his name is that of the prophet John Baptist, who announced the coming of Christ? Was this the introduction to a second book which was to announce his conversion to Christianity and point the way for all of us to understand more deeply and follow more truly the Lord Jesus Christ? We shall never know. Albert Camus was later tragically killed in an automobile wreck. Perhaps it is more probable, as others have suggested, that Jean Baptiste represented the more sophisticated and experienced countries of Europe that have lost the innocent and arrogant vitality of today's younger leaders of the West. They point negatively to what is wrong but contribute nothing to positive solutions in world problems.

Whatever the explanation, this much is true: Jean Baptiste differs in his prophetic approach from John Baptist. The occasion, as distinguished from the cause, of Jean Baptiste's fall was his failure to jump into the Seine to rescue the woman. This scene stands for his failure to enter life with any real participation and giving of himself to any cause or to anyone. All he can do is play roles while he watches life as a spectator unwilling to plunge in. Later the scene of the Seine returns to his conscious mind, and he identifies it with "the bitter water of my baptism" which he never enters.

At the very end of the book he shows himself the conscious parallel to John Baptist but with the fatal difference, ". . . I should have brought to a close, unseen and unknown, my career as a false prophet crying in the wilderness *and refusing to come forth*." *

The baptized Christian follows the prophet *who came forth* from the wilderness and led us to baptism in the living water. The Christian's pride is overcome and transformed by giving himself to the life of Christian service. He does this, by taking each real occasion in his life and placing it in service before God. *The Fall* is not a Christian book and Jean Baptiste is not even a good Jewish prophet, but no Christian will find anywhere a more uncomfortable anatomy of his own pride. It may be that we Christians need to face honestly the sickness of our pride that Camus shows us in the figure Jean Baptiste. Any Christian who criticizes Camus for not being Christian must face the equally serious charge of not living up to that which his own calling entails. At least Jean Baptiste understood the necessity to plunge into the waters of Baptism, even if he could not do it himself. However, the figure of the Cardinal is in stark contrast to that of Jean Baptiste. With all his faults and inadequacies he belongs to a mighty army that is in the midst of baptized life. Insight, cleverness, and profundity are no substitute for the plunge of baptism. And those of us who are Christian need continually to live our baptism, to continue Christ's soldiers and servants until our life's end. The figure of the Cardinal shows us something of what our baptism means in the midst of adversity.

All of us are confronted with experiences not unlike those

* Albert Camus, *The Fall*, trans. by Justin O'Brien (New York: Knopf, 1957), p. 147. (Italics mine.)

of the Cardinal. Perhaps they are not as dramatic, but for us they are no less significant. We, too, have it in our power to take each tragedy, each experience of suffering, as an occasion for compassion, as an opportunity in worship to have our faith more deeply grounded, to recognize our pride, to become more like our humble Lord. As plants grow by the heat of the sun and the drench of showers, so we seem to grow spiritually in the tensions and sufferings and tragedies of our lives. Unlike plants we do not grow spiritually by automatic or mechanical photo-synthesis. We only grow in free choices, in the decisions and experiences of placing our lives, with all their concerns, before our humble Lord. There is nothing that is automatically good about our suffering and tragedy, but at these times we are most likely to see the limitations of our pride and our dependence upon God.

Only those who know something of their own weakness seem to have genuine compassion for others who are weak. The alcoholic is often best helped by members of Alcoholics Anonymous, who have for him that measure of a compassion not found elsewhere. The Cardinal discovered a compassion he had not before possessed when he honestly brought his own agonizing tragedy before the Cross. So with every suffering, frustration, shame, loss of face, and tragedy we too can bring them before the Cross as opportunities of having our pride transformed with the compassion and peace of the humble Christ life. Instead of trying one mighty act of substituting some abstract concept of humility for our pride, we have simply to present our real lives in our present situations in worship. We need not be greedy for opportunities of transforming our pride. There will always be enough frustration and suffering to go around. A member of a Rhodes Scholarship selection board once said that he did not mind a certain cockiness on the part of a twenty-year-old applicant; but if the man were still cocky at thirty, he would be insufferable. There is little opportunity for a person's pride to go unscathed through much of life.

It is in the pinch of pride that is found the opportunity of oblation. Oblation simply means an offering presented in worship. All worship has some oblation, some offering of praise, money, prayer, or things of creation over which God has given us dominion. In the service of Holy Communion we offer oblations of bread and wine. In all worship we should include the bad things as well as the good in our lives so that God may redeem them: all fears, frustrations, shame, indignities, disappointments, and hurt—all the fruits of pride.

Walter Russell Bowie has well expressed in his hymn this continuing opportunity which worship affords us:

> O wounded hands of Jesus, build
>   In us thy new creation;
> Our pride is dust, our vaunt is stilled,
>   We wait thy revelation:
> O love that triumphs over loss,
> We bring our hearts before thy cross,
>   To finish thy salvation.

CHAPTER FIVE

The Fear of Failure

LUCIUS CARY came home from the office one day unusually distraught and upset. Lucius, forty-two years old, with a promising future in his company, faced a dilemma. He was convinced that the newly-announced company policy on bids and sales was dishonest. Should he frankly state his conviction or hold his peace? In the balance hung his possible promotion to the very position that was charged with the execution of this policy. When Lucius explained the situation to his wife Mary, her thoughts immediately raced over their plans for the future: the $2000 a year they needed for four years of college for each child, the new car they had talked about, plus many other things; yet she unhesitatingly replied, "Well, Lucius, you certainly must do what you think is right."

What is right in this situation? What is ethically right for Lucius Cary, his wife, family, and his business? The dilemma of Lucius Cary has its counterpart in countless similar situations the country over. The high school student at a party who, disapproving the behavior, feels faced with deciding whether "to go along" or to state her disapproval and thereby incur rejection is an example. Indeed, agonizing decisions must be made much earlier in life than most adults realize, and life never ceases to present new ones. To do the honest and ethical thing frequently means to threaten one's career and perhaps the status of one's family. The law of society seems to be: success = acceptance; failure = rejection. Indeed, the need to be pleasant, the need we feel to conform, the need to "go along," are all related to our fear of failure.

Fear of failure differs from the other fears we have considered in that it has a negative quality. We should not try to obliterate in worship all fear of failure, but our worship should take away from it that terror and dread whereby the very fear itself contributes to failure and seems to paralyze our wills and courage.

We are also afraid of failure on less obvious and more subtle levels. We are afraid of failing as parents. Do we really feel that we are giving our children what they need in discipline, training, and love for the life in front of them? Often our anxiety over the threat of failing contributes to the greater chance of failure. There seems to be a fine point beyond which the specter of failure paralyzes us. Our lives are certainly more limited and restricted than we realize because of this fear. We waste so much of our lives trying to hedge against possible failure that instead of "getting and spending," the poet could have said, "conforming and fearing we lay waste our powers."

It is not merely an individual matter. Whole communities can become so possessed by fear that they lack the courage and honesty to maintain fairness and justice on community levels. Too many communities take lightly for granted issues of serious social import. Yet the very fabric of civilization rests on courage, the courage to stand and be counted in matters of principle despite threats of failure and rejection.

Decisions involved in these problems require a great wisdom, but wisdom alone does not motivate our actions. We need to overcome our fear of failure in order to know and do what is right. This fear, when present in any enterprise, can be an inhibiting and inertia-producing factor. A student can be so afraid of failing an examination that he "blows up" or "freezes." An athlete can become so tense in his desperate attempt to win that his efficiency is alarmingly impaired. It is interesting to watch professional basketball players take a deep breath and let it out in order to relax their tension before shooting foul shots. In all such situations what is most desperately needed is a way to calm this inhibiting fear of failure without taking away the desire to win or succeed. We all must ask ourselves how we can love life and not fear the things that threaten life? For it is all too easy to drop back into the temptation of ceasing to care—which is the solution of death, not life.

Fear of failure does two things to us. It cuts the nerve of courage to stand for unpopular or uncomfortable positions, and thereby threatens the very integrity of society and ultimately of civilization. It also inhibits our ability to function as effective and real persons in any activity and thereby is a threat to the fullness of life. How then is the fear of failure overcome in worship? This is done in two ways, one rather negative, the other positive.

The first way is simple but uncomfortable. In worship we bring ourselves before the Cross to witness our greatest failure. Any responsible Christian rehearsing the story of the Crucifixion does not present it as a hero story in which "those bad people" kill Christ, with whom we identify. More properly, we see that we are the people who make the suffering necessary and the need for reconciliation. It is we who are alienated from God, ourselves, and from each other. We always seem to need a shock in order to see our own responsibility in any estrangement. This is the problem, the human universal problem, which the Crucifixion answers. Here we see the Son of God take upon himself the hatred and bitterness we creatures show toward God, ourselves, and each other; the very things that cause us to hide from love and create that estrangement which is sin. Christ takes the burden of that estrangement, the feelings and actions which create it, and, without retaliation or threat, he shocks us with his death, the death we have made necessary. Any view of the Cross that does not hold within it one's own culpable involvement is a new Pharisaism, insulating us in tragic self-righteousness from real help and love. We are the people who make innocent suffering necessary. We have already failed the greatest of all tests—the Crucifixion. The remedy of man's inhumanity is found in the true humanity of Christ Jesus. This solution is accomplished in a way to allay our fear, but it can only be understood when we see ourselves as the agents of our predicament.

How does the Crucifixion overcome our fear of failure? To realize that there is no test in the past or future to compare with what we face on Good Friday renders every other test relatively insignificant. Then, to realize in worship before this Incarnation of God's love that we have not passed the test, that we have failed, flunked, "ploughed," renders the threat of any other failure insignificant by comparison. We must see our failure on a much deeper level than a mere academic or intellectual one. In worship we have a dramatic arena in which we can emotionally relive our failure. During the war doctors discovered that it was necessary for shell shock victims to do more than retell their traumatic experiences. They needed to relive them with all the original deep emotional involvement if they were to achieve the catharsis necessary to dispel their vacuous and debilitated condition. Similarly, we need to do more than read a book about our relationship to the Atonement. On Good Friday we must relive with deep emotional involvement our failure in order to dispel that fear of failure which cripples our lives.

When we have really faced our common and tragic failure of this our most important test, we need no longer be inhibited by the fear of any other failure. No test in school, home, office, or life can equal in importance the one we have already "flunked." As Theodore Wedel has frequently put it, "Everybody flunks, but here everybody passes." No one is loved by God because he passed some heavenly college board examination. We pass in spite of our flunking. The only possible response to this news is gratitude. To the extent we hear and know this fact—and in this life it is always a matter of degree—no room remains for envy, ingratitude, bitterness, or self-pity. Can there be room for self-pity when we have earned nothing but rejection and yet have been accepted? Can there be room for envy of outboard motors, houses, and walnut paneling when we deserve nothing and have been given something infinitely better in the demonstrated love of our Father Creator? Can there be room for bitterness when our deepest bitterness has been taken and swallowed up in a death a thousand times more unjust than any injustice we have ever felt?

The glorious emancipation in facing, in three dimensions, this our greatest failure provides us with a strong heat-forged, cauterized basis for our lives which need never be overcome by fear of any other failure. A hunter tells of an experience while shooting ducks in an abandoned rice field overgrown by reeds and rushes taller than a man. The party of three saw a wisp of smoke on the horizon but thought no more about it in the excitement of the hunt until they noticed a noise that kept growing louder and nearer. A fire was burning through the rushes, and the intense and sudden heat was turning the water in the reeds to steam, and, one by one, the reeds were exploding, and the explosions drawing ever nearer. The hunters, heavily clothed and wearing hip boots, sank, at every step, to their knees in mud. There was no possible way to outrun the fire. Suddenly one of the men took out his cigarette lighter and lit a small pile of brush close by. Another exclaimed, "Haven't we enough fire without your starting more?" But the words were hardly out of his mouth when he saw the meaning of the small fire. It made a thin strip of burned-over land beyond which they were able to take refuge, safe from the roaring flames. For us the Crucifixion can be that burned-over place which gives us somewhere to stand, instead of running in panic from the engulfing fires of life's failures.

In William Inge's play *Dark at the Top of the Stairs*, there is one character who shows unusual courage in the face of small threats because of the suffering he has previously endured on much deeper levels. Sammy, a Jewish boy at the local academy, is Rennie's blind date. When he arrives in the parlor, everyone is exceedingly uncomfortable, fearful, and somewhat embarrassed. Sammy immediately perceives this and alleviates their fear. Sammy's concern and sensitivity evoke from both Rennie and her younger brother a warm response, and they began to feel at great ease with him. At the dance Sammy is quite rudely and cruelly hurt when the hostess' mother points out that Jews are not welcome. He rushes away and, in the play, jumps to his death from the fourteenth floor of his hotel. The next day's scene is one in which the brother and sister hear the news of the death of this person who had cared for them, and they see each other in a new and wonderful way that effects a most credible reconciliation. Here is a rough example of how a third person enters a relationship where estrangement is present, evokes affections and trust, dies innocently, and leaves the remaining partners looking over his grave with a measure of their fear buried. They see each other differently now, having shared a mutual suffering; and this new understanding and compassion heals their estrangement in a rough but meaningful way.

The role of this Jewish boy as an instrument of reconciliation roughly parallels that of Jesus, as Professor Davy Napier and others have observed. It is a crude analogy, but it does point to a crucial element of the Atonement. Human situations that need reconciliation and atonement are situations in which love can neither be given nor received, because both parties feel the need to defend themselves from hurt by the other. Vicious circles of hurt, created in fact by the very fear of being hurt, are only broken by a love that is willing to suffer, for it alone can pierce the veils of fear. Those who respond to the innocent and vulnerable love that knows hurt and willingly dies are never the same. To respond to this kind of love is to participate in its hurt and in its death, just as Rennie and her brother, having participated in Sammy's love, also participated in his death. Death is the terrible cost that love pays to effect reconciliation and atonement, indeed to win us. And this sacrificial cost is made necessary by our estrangement and our fear. This is our great failure. Squarely facing this failure in worship overcomes all terror of any subsequent failure. The fear of failure is buried in this terrible judgment. When this failure is taken as the very banner behind which the Christian Church marches, when the instrument of death can be drawn in water on our foreheads at baptism, when God can take this failure and make it the means of a new creation, what terror can any other test then have?

The examples of both the Cardinal and Stypulkowski show the power of such burned-over experiences. Stypulkowski did not need to hide from his inadequacies because he had already seen them in this terrible judgment of the Cross and realized that Christ had justified him. The Cardinal's courage to explore every possible avenue of weakness and failure in himself, which so profoundly impressed the interrogator, was certainly related to, and stemmed from, the Cardinal's grounding in that great failure before the Cross. St. Paul's awareness of his role in persecuting Christ ("Saul, Saul, why persecutest thou me") was the springboard into his new life. Indeed, an astonishing aspect of St. Paul's new life was his understanding of how God takes our very weaknesses to make us strong. Every failure in life can become the weakness through which God can work, as he told St. Paul, "My strength is made perfect in weakness." (II Cor. 12:9) Out of the Cardinal's failure in prison arose the deeper qualities of peace and compassion. In facing ever more deeply our greatest of all failures, our failure before God in making it necessary for Christ to suffer and die to redeem us, we establish a basis upon which debilitating fears of subsequent failures are taken away and each actual failure and weakness is an occasion for God to make us strong. This, too, is a continual and ever deepening experience of worship in which we involve ourselves more and more in the response to God's love in Christ.

One of the profoundest themes of our Christian faith is that we die with Christ in his death. This is the meaning of our Baptism, that we die to sin. Especially on Good Friday, but also in every service of Holy Communion, we behold him in his death and in responsive worship participate in that death. All the pus of bitterness, self-pity, resentment, and fear is drawn out of us, when in true worship we put ourselves before the magnetic expression of God's love in the death of his Son upon the cross. "We bring ourselves before thy cross to finish thy salvation." Our fears are pierced by this example of helpless, non-threatening love nailed to a tree; all the poison of sin is destroyed and buried as we participate through worship in his death.

St. Bernard instructs us on the four stages in the Christian life of true worship. In the first stage *we love man for man's sake*. Undeniably, there is in man some measure of love for man, his fellow, whether he be Christian or not. It may not be sufficient or adequate, but it is a mistake to deny that a measure of such love has and does exist in mankind. The second stage is the seemingly logical one that most of us have made: *we love God for man's sake*. It is not difficult to see man's terrible failures on the first level, man's inhumanity to man throughout history and now. Therefore, we as Christians can easily understand the second stage, how we must love God for man's sake. We need to have churches, Christian education, worship, and Christian institutions to teach and show how we must love each other. And this second stage is one which most of us reach. But having reached this stage, let us not forget that we are loving God as a means, an instrument, for the love of man. Indeed, we can substitute self for man: we love God for our own sake. Of course, God is no mere means to gain good ends. He is the End; he is the Alpha and Omega. But God can only be a means if our purposes, our ends, our hopes and desires, are the ends and purpose of our worship. Moreover, when we sometimes love our family or an institution for its own sake, any threat is an ultimate threat and makes us touchy, defensive, frantic, or bitter.

The third stage is the hardest, and one too few Christians attain: *we love God for God's sake*. In other words, here we let go. We love God not for the sake of "St. John's" Church, Christian education, the peace of the world, or an institution no matter how great. We love God not in order that we may become better husbands or wives or parents. We love God not in order that our fears may be overcome and cast out, or that we may be fulfilled. We simply cut loose from all to love God *for his sake alone*. At this stage we die not only to sin and to all the evil in us; we die completely. We die to the good things, great hopes, compassion for hurt, indignation before injustice, dreams of peace, and hope of salvation. We let loose and soar. We leave even the love of family, of church, of country, western civilization, and the future of humanity. *We love God for God's sake*. This is the great divide. Most of us who call ourselves Christian really love God for the sake of all the good things we believe in and for the sake of our children and of our wives. But these good things must be given up, must be given up as ends and as reasons for our love of God. We must die to self and be buried with Christ. We must cut lose and quite simply, but quite totally, *love God for God's sake*.

The fourth stage is reached when we return, as Jesus did

with Peter, James, and John, from the Mount of Transfiguration into the arena of history: when *we love man for God's sake*. Now we care for all the good things of western civilization, our three-year-old daughter—yes, even our new pair of shoes. We work and hope and pray, we care for all things and all people for God's sake. We need not fear now to hope or love or care too much, because in hoping, caring, and loving for God's sake nothing is finally lost or defeated or killed. Here we can see the power of the Gospel in the words of Jesus: "He that loveth father or mother more than me is not worthy of me and he that loveth son or daughter more than me is not worthy of me . . . He that findeth his life shall lose it: and he that loseth his life *for my sake* shall find it." (Matt. 10:37-39, italics mine) Seen in the context of worship this is not a hard saying but a glorious one. Who has not seen a young mother afraid of loving her son too much because she knows she must one day lose him? None of us is aware of how much we unconsciously withdraw from love, hope, people, country, good aims, because the threat of caring too much leaves us poignantly vulnerable to the hurt of failure or loss. Jesus is not telling us to love our parents or children less, but he is showing us how we can love them more. He is not telling us to care less about life and our hopes. Instead, he is showing how we can find our lives by losing them in him.

We worship, therefore, not to cast out our fear. We worship to cast ourselves loose from the ties of self. Every act of worship should be a reminder of this good news of our death. In confession and thanksgiving we offer ourselves, the bad and the good, to God for his sake. Especially in the Lord's Supper, in the memorial, in the recollection or anamnesis of the death of Christ, we participate in his death and live our baptism, our death to self and our new life in Christ.

When we find our new life at this fourth stage, we find that we are baptized into a fellowship, into a body of newborn people called the Church. Here we see that each is not the same, and that our unity is not gained through conformity but through the common tasks and citizenship of the kingdom of God. The tasks are quite different, but we are reminded by St. Paul that the body has many members. "For as the body is one, and hath many members, and all the members of that one body, being many, are one body: so also is Christ." (I Cor. 12:12)

We are now at the place where we can profitably re-examine the dilemma of Lucius Cary. What should Lucius do? Should he compromise his ethics for the sake of his career and his family's livelihood? Or should he "make no peace with oppression" and protest whatever is not ethical, regardless of the consequences? First of all, no one can tell Lucius what to do; his decision must be his own. No one can make it for him or take the responsibility for it. There are, however, several things to ask. What course will be most effective? What is the end and motive and purpose of any decision? It might be that, as a Christian loving man for God's sake, he can see that the thing to do is live with no compromise in the company. On the other hand, he may decide that this matter is not one sufficiently important to "go to the stake" for, so to speak. Many situations in life must be lived with simply because the alternatives are worse or because of the sheer impossibility of altering the situation now in any basic way. In this generation we do not have an option of living in a world without Red China. There are no perfect businesses or people. We need the wisdom to know what can be changed, and the grace to change those things that can be changed.

This situation and all others for which it stands, however, can be put in the new context on this side of our Good Friday. We are now part of a community, a corporate society and everything that affects one member affects the whole. Lucius Cary is not in this situation by himself. As Christians, it is our dilemma too. Though no one can make the decision *for* him, he makes it *with* the whole Church. All guilt is ultimately corporate guilt. We share in it and in its solution. The whole enterprise of the Christian is involved in, and responsible for, Lucius Cary's dilemma. He does not face this alone. He is not faced with only two alternatives. God does not put ethical demands upon a man in a spiritually tight compartment. Cary lives with his agonizing decisions in an organism that shares in the responsibility to rectify, wisely, powerfully, and in charity, any injustice. Therefore, what do *we* do about Lucius Cary's problem? It may be that the wisest and most effective way of redeeming the situation is to bring pressure from the outside, frequently through already existing means in the structure of our society. We are also reminded that functions differ. "And the eye cannot say unto the hand, I have no need of thee . . ." (I Cor. 12:21) There are varying gifts of the spirit and differing vocations in the body. Some are called to be prophets, and some teachers. Unfortunately, Christians sometime forget their corporate nature and fail to realize that we do not all have the same vocations. In one part of the South a very liberal and outspoken clergyman says things about the race problem which if said by most clergy would destroy their pastoral relationship with their congregations. One wise minister said that although he disagreed with his outspoken colleague he found that having him in the vicinity made it easier for him to take a more effective moderate stand. It is not given to all to do the same thing. We should be more grateful for our outspoken prophets and more understanding of those not so outspoken, realizing the while that as a corporate society, we are responsible. Therefore, we are not merely presented with an individual alternative. We can decide not to be a prophet, but to participate in another's prophecy through our common corporate society. We do not fight injustice in society in lonely decisions but by being a part of, and participating in, the social responsibilities of the corporate Church.

Surely, one of the great weaknesses of the Christian's witness in the community is that he mistakenly believes that he is alone with these dilemmas. He thinks that if he has compromised in business, he is not really a Christian and is a hypocrite in going to church. Many laymen seem to think that children, women, and clergy are the only ones so far removed from agonizing compromises that only they can enter the church pure and morally clean. In fact, children, women, clergy, and even monks, are continually faced with situations frequently no more subtle or less sinful than a businessman faces. Also, if a man out of weakness does not do what he knows he should, this is not the end. If one is weak, one is weak; and this is a fact we must face to be strong. He who has compromised his integrity has plenty of company in church. Our guilt is common and corporate; and when offered in confession it is absolved with power. This power can be much more effectively trained upon the world for justice when we realize its corporate nature. The doctor's agonizing decisions involving suffering and life, the high school student's dilemma in courtship problems, the newsstand operator's indecision about what to sell, the lawyer's problem of how to defend his client, and the scholar's use of sources, all are our mutual problems and must be solved by us as the Body that we are.

Here we see another and more positive way in which our fears are overcome. We have not only died to sin, we have been reborn in his kingdom. This is well expressed by a phrase in the General Thanksgiving prayer, "by giving up ourselves to thy service . . ." Our fears of failure are overcome not only by having this "burned-over" place in our lives but by having our lives themselves taken up into the kingdom of God. "Seek ye first the kingdom of God and all these things shall be added unto you." To be a part of God's kingdom is to be where nothing ultimately fails but sin. The life of worship is one that continually is given up to God's service.

This idea is a singularly unpopular one today, but perhaps that is the malady of our times: we are self-oriented. "Doesn't every woman have a right to happiness?" asks a recent soap opera. "Read the Bible and acquire peace of mind." Because "the family that prays together stays together," church is a good thing. We are frequently told that Christianity is important because it helps combat Communism. Sometimes we are told that the Bible and Christianity are helpful for our emotional problems. In other words, most of what we are told about Christianity puts the cart before the horse. We are presented such good things as Christianity, the Bible, the Church and worship, as things by which we may gain our own ends. Prayer is portrayed as though it were some heavenly room service. We put God in the role of some sort of celestial "bellboy."

We may not feel that these crude analyses apply to us, but in some degree we are inevitably involved in using our religion to fulfill our wills rather than to change and redeem them. The real irony is that God's will for us is so much better than our own. St. Augustine's mother earnestly and devoutly prayed that her son not leave North Africa for Rome, where she thought it less likely that he would be converted. At the very time she was on her knees in church her son was boarding ship for Rome. The form of Monica's prayer was denied in order that the real content be granted, and it was on this trip from North Africa that Augustine was converted. A happily married man with three children admits that one of the greatest disappointments of his life was that a thirty-four-year-old widow would not marry him when he was eighteen years old and a soldier in Japan. He says now, "Well, let's see, I'm thirty-four now. That would make her just fifty. I'm certainly grateful that God has not given me what I wanted!"

Christian worship is not food for our wills but an enterprise in which we continue to give our whole selves to God and his will in his kingdom. When this is done, and to the extent that it is done, our failures are relegated to two categories: failures that should fail and desires that need judgment and correction, and failures of good things that will ultimately triumph and out of which failures even greater good can be born. This is a by-product of giving one's entire self to God's service. The simple meaning of Baptism is to know through worship that nothing good ultimately fails.

In the middle of the second century some unknown Christian expressed this quality of Christian membership in the kingdom of God in a document called "Letter to Diognetus":

For Christians cannot be distinguished from the rest of the human race by country or language or customs. They do not live in cities of their own; they do not use a peculiar form of speech; they do not follow an eccentric manner of life. This doctrine of theirs has not been discovered by the ingenuity or deep thought of inquisitive men, nor do they put forward a merely human teaching, as some people do. Yet, although they live in Greek and barbarian cities alike, as each man's lot has been cast, and follow the customs of the country in clothing and food and other matters of daily living, at the same time they give proof of the remarkable and admittedly extraordinary constitution of their own commonwealth. They live in their own countries, but only as aliens. They have a share in every thing as citizens, and endure everything as foreigners. Every foreign land is their fatherland, and yet for them every fatherland is a foreign land. They marry, like everyone else, and they beget children, but they do not cast out their offspring. They share their board with each other, but not their marriage bed. It is true that they are "in the flesh," but they do not live "according to the flesh." They busy themselves on earth, but in their own lives they go far beyond what the laws require. They love all men, and by all men are persecuted. They are unknown, and still they are condemned; they are put to death, and yet they are brought to life. They are poor, and yet they make many rich; they are completely destitute, and yet they enjoy complete abundance. They are dishonored, and in their very dishonor are glorified; they are defamed, and are vindicated. They are reviled, and yet they bless; when they are affronted, they still pay due respect. When they do good, they are punished as evildoers; undergoing punishment, they rejoice because they are brought to life.*

* "Letter to Diognetus," translated by E. R. Fairweather, in *Early Christian Fathers,* edited by C. C. Richardson (London: S.C.M. Press), vol. I.

CHAPTER SIX

The Fear of Being Human

WE SHOULD meet Jimmy Porter because in knowing and understanding him we understand something of the fear of being human. Jimmy, a character in John Osborne's play *Look Back in Anger*, is married to an upper-class girl named Alison and they live in a one-room flat in the midlands of England. At first glance this play seems to be no more than a rude protest against the rigid class lines of contemporary English society, but a more careful look opens up a real depth of insight into the human predicament. Throughout much of the play Alison is standing over an ironing board in a white slip. She is blond, wears no make-up, and gives the impression of death in the midst of life. She is accused by Jimmy of being sycophantic, phlegmatic, and pusillanimous. The latter word he takes great pleasure in defining: "wanting of firmness of mind, of small courage, having a little mind, mean spirited, cowardly, timid of mind." Alison seems to represent the stoic retreat from life. The underlying assumption of the play is expressed in the repeated phrase, "the pain of being human." This pain is so great that Alison retreats from it in a kind of "novacained," zombie-like existence of walking death. Her condition is expressed by the classical stoic, almost casual, remark, "If you continue to twist my arm you'll break it." In order to stand the pain the stoic dissociates himself from his body (and his life), regarding it as some impersonal object external to himself. Historically, the stoic ethic has been one of the most noble; but a great price is paid for this sort of heroism, the price of involvement, caring, and living.

Jimmy Porter believes that the "pain of being human" is too great to bear. Because we are human, we are free; and because we are free, we must decide; and because we must decide, we are anxious. Nothing produces anxiety more than the necessity to make decisions. The freedom involved in being human, therefore, results in our chronic, frustrating anxiety. As if this were not enough, being human inevitably involves being guilty. If we are truly human we are truly free; and if we are free, we are responsible; and if we are responsible, we are guilty. Jimmy's solution is in the opposite direction of stoicism. His is in the direction of the squirrels and bears. Animals, being amoral and nonhuman, are not plagued with the dilemma and pain of being human. They are neither anxious nor guilty.

The deadness of Alison's alternative to being human irritates and distresses Jimmy. He tries by insult and injury to make her respond, to fight, cry, or do anything that will show that she is not pusillanimous but alive. They can only be happy, significantly enough, as they play a rough little game in which she is a squirrel and he, a bear. In his desperate attempt to blast her out of her stoic sepulchre, he is viciously ugly and insulting. He describes her brother as a frightened phony, and her mother as a rhinoceros in labor. He is crude and cruel, with real imagination. He is so inhuman to her that critics of the play have gotten so lost in the action as to insist that he should be spanked!

John Osborne seems to be telling us that because of anxiety and guilt the pain of being human is so great that we have only two alternatives. We may, like Alison, retreat from life into a shell of protection behind which we are not hurt because we no longer feel. Or we may shake our fist at the phony standards of society and ethics, and live the life of amoral animals, immune to the painful anxiety and guilt of being human. In the play Jimmy finally succeeds in hurting Alison so badly that she does come out of her sepulchre of retreat with tears and expressions of agony. Jimmy then holds her tenderly and says that they can now love each other again. She can be the squirrel and he, the bear. The curtain comes down on two frightened humans trying to squeeze some painless life out of a game of being animals.

This play is no isolated example of this view of life. Among others, Eric Fromm has written lucidly on our desire to escape the anxiety of freedom in his book *Escape from Freedom*; and Oskar Pfister, in *Fear and Christianity*, has written learnedly on the destructive power of the guilt that arises from freedom. Another clue to the relevance of this play to our times and our lives is Jimmy Porter's grudging admiration of Alison's father, who is a relic of the Edwardian era. He is willing to grant that despite its phony red coats and starched linen, the Edwardian society was at least alive. In this generation there is a rude protest to the lifelessness of society and its conventions by the beatniks, who being "beat"

have little to lose in venturing into some sort of amoral existence. In England the young protesting generation called
"teddy-boys," whose clothes seek to copy the Edwardian
dress, seem to reflect Jimmy Porter's grudging admiration
for the confident Engishmen at the turn of the century. But
characteristically, their protest is in the amoral form expressed by Jimmy in his animal and essentially nonhuman
alternative.

Here we can see something of why we are afraid to be
truly human. Jimmy Porter is certainly right that being human is a painful enterprise. Our reactions to the fear of being
human may not be as dramatic as Alison's and Jimmy's, but
the deeply emotional reactions of the sophisticated playgoers
who saw this play are a testimony to its relevance. (Many
wanted to beat up Jimmy Porter, and others were alarmingly
gleeful in their enjoyment of Jimmy's cruelty.) Possibly it
can be said that the play represents, despite its exaggerations,
the options of the non-Christian world to our fear of being
human. What is the Christian option? How is our fear of
being human overcome in worship?

The first way in which our worship overcomes this fear is
by looking again at Christ whom we follow. One of the ways
we can see something new in his humanity is by asking ourselves St. Augustine's tricky question: "Is it better to be able
not to sin or not to be able to sin?" Or, to put it another way,
"Was Christ able not to sin or not able to sin?" We need to
safeguard carefully that full and real humanity which was
"in all points tempted like we are, yet without sin." Christ
was neither a dehydrated human nor some being between the
levels of God and man. He was both fully God and fully man.
However, the text certainly does not mean that Christ was
tempted with the particular sins which tempt us. Many temp-

tations which you and I know are the result of sin and guilt which Christ did not know. One clergyman says that in the beginning of his ministry he handled all pastoral problems with the question, "What would Jesus have done?" Finally one man replied, "But, sir, Jesus would never have gotten himself in the situation I'm in."

If we say that it is better to be able not to sin, do we really mean that Jesus wanted to do all the things we want to do but was able to grit his teeth, hold himself down, suppress his desires, and was thus able not to sin? On the other hand, have we not known people who were morally incapable of being tempted on certain crude levels? Are not some actions morally impossible for certain people? Would you prefer a wife who was able not to sin, or not able to sin in the form of chopping your head off with an axe? Surely we would feel more comfortable knowing that she is morally unable to kill with an axe rather than feeling that, though she wanted to do so, she steeled herself and was able to refrain from doing it.

Years ago there was a movie, starring Ray Milland, called *Alias Nick Beal.* Milland as Nick was helping an honest judge campaign for governor against a corrupt machine. As the movie developed, it became apparent that Nick was Nicholas Beelzebub, the devil, who was attempting subtly to capture the soul of the judge. Nick needed to separate the judge from his wife, and for that purpose installed a secretary in his office to break up the marriage. At one crucial moment when the judge was going to see his secretary at her apartment, Nick Beal arrives first to see that everything is set up to tempt the judge. The secretary is in a slinky dress, the lights are down low, music is playing, and whisky is on the coffee table. Nick is furious. He tells her to put on a tweed suit, take the whisky away, and should the judge ask for any, to tell him that no liquor is kept in her apartment. As Nick points out, the judge is too fine a man to be tempted on crude levels. He can only be tempted on more subtle levels which are clothed in the confusing appearance of wholesomeness and respectability. There are always different levels of temptation for different people.

It is exceedingly important to see Christ not as a five-star Sunday School puritan who is able to climb on top of his temptations and hold them down with tense rigidity and gritted teeth. This is no picture of the incarnate Lord and perfect humanity. Instead, we see Christ tempted in terms of his kingdom. As he shows us our true humanity, we must see ourselves not as putting a lid on our desires and temptations but as being changed inside so that we love what God wills. As St. Augustine said, "We love God and do as we please." Our fear of being human is not resolved by being dead, by becoming merely animal, or by clamping down and repressing our inclinations. Our true humanity is to be seen in Jesus Christ, who was so free that he was morally not able to be bound. As sin is the bondage of man and his separation from his true nature, man's aim is not to sit on top of his sin but to be rid of it altogether. Our fear of being human is overcome in worship by having our wills and desires, our fears and ourselves, changed and made more human, not less so.

In overcoming our fear of being human we must understand the reality expressed by the words, body and blood and sacrifice. When Jesus uses the terms "body and blood" and when the New Testament speaks of sacrifices, the long experience and history of the Jewish people is assumed. In order to understand these apparently simple terms we must know what the writers of the New Testament meant by them. To begin with, the Hebrew understood something about God that many Christians seem to forget. God is of "purer eyes than to behold iniquity." Jehovah of Israel was thought of neither as a big strong heavenly Hebrew nor as an indulgent grandfather. He was seen as the absolutely righteous God of creation. It has been said that God created man in his own image and now man seeks to return the compliment. But the Hebrew people knew better than to try to make God over in their image. Even Moses was unable to see God face to face and, when confronted by Jahweh, had to hide in a cleft of the rock with his back turned. (Ex. 33: 20-23)

If God could not be approached and addressed casually because of his righteousness and man's iniquity, then how could it be possible to communicate with him? The Hebrew people, with profound religious insight, took an animal, often a lamb, and used the innocency of the lamb as a vehicle of communication with God. The animal being amoral had not sinned and, therefore, possessed the required innocency necessary to enter the presence of God. The Hebrew also understood something that we are apt to miss. Deism of the eighteenth century may have taught us to think of creation as that which took place and was completed long ago. The Hebrew, however, understood the eternal immediacy of creation. All creation exists at any moment because it is being sustained by God's power. Creation is not finished; it has only begun and is being continued. Therefore, the Hebrew saw food in a particularly religious context. Food that is grown and provided by God is a medium of his action in the continuing creation of nurture and sustenance. This is a nurture of the spirit as well as the body. Thus, God gives man animals for food, and in eating this food the Hebrew had a very religious experience. We ignore this insight today to our great detriment, but even in the twentieth century we seem to realize something deeply intangible about eating.

We receive love and care at the beginning of our lives in association with eating. We are cared for as we are nurtured and fed. We seem to be more vulnerable to love when we are eating. It is a custom of our culture to choose someone we particularly care for with whom to dine. Look at the number of eating clubs and the amount of fellowship over food which occurs in church, business, social, and community organizations. We all seem to appreciate something intangibly significant about the association of love and fellowship with the act of eating food. Of course, when we are vulnerable to love, we are at the same time vulnerable to hurt. Eating in an unpleasant atmosphere can be quite harmful, not only in an obvious physical sense, but also in an emotional sense, as when fear and resentment are ingested along with the food. Hence, the influences present at meal time, that vulnerable and spiritually contagious arena, are of extreme importance.

The Hebrew not only understood this in the very meaningful religious context of his relation with God who continuously creates him physically and spiritually, but he also understood what we often fail to see. The attitude of the people of Israel toward bodies was in marked contrast with the general tendency of Greek civilization. The Jew knew he was created in the image of God and that God saw what he had made and called it good. The Hebrew knew that sin could not simply be blamed upon his body. However, the Platonic, neo-Platonic and later Eastern philosophies encouraged us to use our bodies as scapegoats. It is this so-called Greek influence that has given us the idea that our spirits are good and our bodies are bad. (St. Paul does not mean this by his contrast between the flesh and the spirit.) The Hebrew knew that the body is necessary to manifest spirit. We would not know each other, were it not for our bodies.

This relation is well observed in a passage from the philosopher William Ernest Hocking.

I have sometimes sat looking at a comrade, speculating on this mysterious isolation of self from self. Why are we so made that I gaze and see of thee only thy Wall and never thee? This Wall of thee is but a movable part of the Wall of my world; and I also am a Wall to thee: we look out at one another from behind masks. How would it seem if my mind could but once be *within* thine; and we could meet and without barrier be with each other? And then it has fallen upon me like a shock—as when one thinking himself alone has felt a presence— But I *am* in thy soul. These things around me are in thy experience. They are thy own; when I touch them and move them I change thee. When I look on them I see what thou seest; when I listen, I hear what thou hearest. I am in the great Room of thy soul; and I experience thy very experience. For *where art thou?* Not there, behind those eyes, within that head, in darkness, fraternizing with chemical processes. Of these, in my own case, I know nothing, and will know nothing; for my existence is spent not behind my Wall, but in front of it. I am there, where I have treasures. And there art thou, also. This world in which I live, is the world of thy soul: and being within that, I am within thee. I can imagine no contact more real and thrilling than this; that we should meet and share identity, not through ineffable inner depths (alone), but here through the foregrounds of common experience; and that thou shouldst be—not behind that mask —but *here,* pressing with all thy consciousness upon me, *containing me,* and these things of mine. This is reality: and having seen it thus, I can never again be frightened into monadism by reflections which have strayed from their guiding insight.

Any connecting medium is apt to appear as an obstacle to direct relationship; on the other hand any obstacle may discover itself to be a mediator, sign of unbroken continuity. The sea separates—or the sea connects; it cannot do one without doing the other also. So Nature *may be* interpreted in its relation to social consciousness, as the visible pledge and immediate evidence of our living contact. If there be any social consciousness, it must include within itself just such physical appearances as we have been reviewing, even in its ideal perfection.*

The Hebrew also knew that bodies were the means of communication. He took a lamb that was acceptable to God because of its innocency and offered it to God, among other reasons, as a means of communication and communion. The lamb was a part of creation, and as man ate of the lamb God sustained, nurtured, and continued his creation. Offering a particular lamb to God and eating it in a religious context provided an atmosphere in which God's fellowship and love could be communicated with eating this food.

We come now to the point of the blood. To kill the lamb it was stuck with a knife and bled until dead. As long as the lamb shed blood, it was alive; only when the bleeding stopped, was it dead. Naturally the people of Israel regarded blood as the life of the lamb. Perhaps now we can see what our Lord meant about the cup. James and John had asked him about being on his right and left side in the kingdom. Jesus replied with the question, "Can you drink of my cup?" In the Garden of Gethsemane Jesus prayed that this cup be allowed to pass from his lips. What does he mean by this cup? What is in the cup? He tells us at the Last Supper, "This is my blood which is shed for you. Do this in remembrance of me." Here, as "the lamb of God that taketh away the sins of the world," his blood is his *life outpoured*. If we

* W. E. Hocking, *The Meaning of God in Human Experience* (New Haven: Yale University Press, 1912) p. 265.

are squeamish about the word "blood" in the Lord's Supper, we can substitute the word "life," but let us remember that it means *life outpoured*. "This is my blood which is shed for you." The emphasis is on the verb "shed."

Now we can understand something else Jesus said. "He took bread and when he had given thanks he brake it and gave it to his disciples, saying, 'Take, eat, this is my Body which is given for you.'" "This is my Body." Here Jesus pours out his life and leaves us a body which fulfills the purpose of communication. The Epistle to the Hebrews reminds us that as God spoke in times past through prophets, he has now spoken to us in his Son. The Word of God incarnate was the body by which he spoke. His historical body is no longer with us, but he left a body through which we may continue to communicate with him. He uses the food of the supper and sets it aside, identifying his blood with the cup and his body with the breaking and eating of the bread.

Dr. A. T. Mollegen offers an analogy that is helpful in understanding something of the communication of the Supper. We must recall that our bodies are means of communication through quite physical media: lungs, vocal cords, tongue, teeth, and lips, vibrating air, ears, and brain. All these physical things are means whereby we know and are known. Sometimes, however, we are so far removed in distance that we cannot shout across the space that divides us. The telephone provides a physical means of communicating over distances that would otherwise separate us. A father leaves home and travels five hundred miles to a distant city. He picks up the telephone and calls home. He uses his body in the same way he would in natural conversation, but this time he speaks into a gadget which translates the vibrations of his physical body into electrical current traveling at the rate of

186,300 miles per second which is then retranslated into audible vibrations to the ear of his daughter, who has answered the telephone. She in turn calls her mother saying, "Daddy's on the phone." Now they do not sit down to argue whether Daddy is inside the telephone, on top of the telephone, or if he is the telephone. They simply use this physical extention of his body to receive his presence in communication with him.

In a very rough way this is analogous to Christ's being where we need another means of communicating with him. As he showed himself in his physical body when he was in his earthly ministry, now he shows himself in the breaking of the bread. The broken bread and the broken body, the wine outpoured and the blood shed, the innocent victim and the victorious sacrifice is the food of Christians.

This brings us to the third word "sacrifice." In any other context sacrifice seems to mean loss, as the sacrifice of a car or business. Here there is a giving up, but this loss becomes fulfillment in Christianity. We have seen that an offering in worship is called an oblation. An oblation that is fulfilled in its offering is a sacrifice. Olive Wyon helpfully illustrates the relationship of oblation to sacrifice. An arrow shot from a bow is like an oblation when it is in the air. When it quivers home in the target, it is like a sacrifice. Oblations are offerings directed toward their destination. When they are gathered up in their final destiny, there is a sacrifice. Christ completed his offered life on a cross and was raised from the dead; this was his fulfillment and sacrifice. As we offer ourselves to God in the breaking of bread and are accepted in Christ, we are where we were intended to be, we are "home," we are fulfilled. This is our sacrifice.

Thus our worship allows God's love to overcome our fear

of being human. We not only become like Christ by be-holding him but also by eating of his body in this thanksgiving feast. A story of a family automobile accident illustrates quite well something of the nature of our participation in this feast. An accident occurred in a rural county and the family was taken to a small hospital. Fortunately, no one was badly hurt except the little girl. She had lost a great deal of blood, and the hospital did not have the type she needed for transfusion. Her small brother was the only immediate source of the necessary kind of blood. The doctor suggested to her father that he ask the boy to give some of his blood to his sister. He went out to a car where the boy was waiting and told him that his sister was quite ill and asked if he would give her a transfusion. The boy replied that he would and walked back into the hospital with his father. They came down a hall, into the treatment room where his sister was, and a nurse helped him onto a table next to her. Since he was young and might wiggle about with the needle in his arm, the doctor decided to put him to sleep while the transfusion was in process. As his blood went into his sister her color returned and she began to recover. Later, as he was waking up, his father came into the room. He looked down at his son and said, "Son, I just want to thank you for giving some of your blood to your sister." Looking up from his pillow the boy replied, "My blood? I thought I was gonna give my life."

Here is an example of our childlike willingness to care which, though buried, can be recovered in our life of worship. As we drink of his cup, "we offer ourselves, our souls, and bodies to be a reasonable (human, not animal), holy, and living (not dead) sacrifice unto thee." This sacrifice is not loss but fulfillment. The words "reasonable" and "living" are in contrast to the Old Testament "animal" and "dead";

115

they are also in contrast to Jimmy Porter's animal, and Alison's dead, alternatives. Here then, in our participation in the Holy Communion, our fear of being human is overcome and we are fed the food to become more deeply and completely human.

CHAPTER SEVEN

The Fear of Love

OUR FEAR of love is not always immediately apparent. To love and be loved is what we all think we want, but there is a great price to be paid in any such relationship. There are few of us who are not dimly aware of a stubborn and deep reluctance to love. Love is a threat to our self-will. Love involves us in a relationship of compromise and sacrifice, thoughtfulness and consideration of others, new contingencies and dependencies, all of which represent radical qualifications upon our self-will. How our money and time are spent, what kind of tooth paste we use or what movie we attend, what color draperies or what kind of breakfast cereal we choose, are all relatively simple matters in our isolation and independence. But loving another person inevitably makes even these simple choices matters of alarming complexity, fraught with probabilities of real anguish. Tops are not replaced on tooth paste tubes. Money is spent on golf clubs instead of a new rug, and one's life is simply not his own in a relationship of love. If a friend is sick it is a demand on our time, our thoughts, and upon our very life. Thus, love is a threat to our freedom. Our life is not our own unless we are independent, and our time and desires are not contingent upon the time and desires of others. The unhampered exercise of our own wills is thus radically threatened when we enter into close association with another person.

Of course, there is another side. Our wills desire community and other people. We do realize that the absolute independence of the hermit is no splendid isolation. Hence, each of us is involved in some in-between measure of independence, qualified with compromises that seem worth the community of association. In other words, we may fully realize the inconveniences incumbent upon us in loving another person, but the loss of freedom may be considered worth the gain of fellowship. Any friendship or marriage has an element of this consideration in it. If, however, this is all it amounts to—a chronic cold war or reluctant and constant compromise—it is only a most embryonic form of love. It is a kind of love of the market place, one of bargains and trades, sanctions and liens, debts and payments. Here our self-will understands the need for some compromise and carefully contrives to get the most possible for whatever must be sacrificed in the way of qualifications on the self-will. When love grows beyond that point, it becomes a serious threat to independence. To leave the level of bargaining is to arrive at that of giving, giving of oneself, of one's will, time, desires, freedom, and independence. This not only involves experiences of hurt and mutual suffering, but our wills and lives become inextricably tied up with the wills and lives of others.

Consequently, no one can hurt us quite as much as those

we love. "You always hurt the one you love, the one you shouldn't hurt at all," is the way an old song puts it. The closeness of love reveals a vulnerability to hurt and a threat to our self-centeredness. Two or more self-centered people thrown close together can produce tragedy and suffering not possible in real isolation. Much of the sadness involved in love is a sadness related to hurt in the conflict of wills at close quarters. "The song of love is a sad song. Don't ask me how I know." Anyone who has ever loved can sing this along with Lili and in some real measure understand that the song of love is indeed a sad song. We have developed so many subtle and clever ways of living in the midst of people, while retaining our isolation, that we tend to forget how threatening it is to be really close to someone else. Self-will is a thorny instrument, blunt and safe in isolation, but in the closeness of love dangerous and capable of inflicting serious hurt. Love is a radical threat to us, and deep-down it is human to fear it.

Love presents yet another threat to our condition that is more serious than either the threat of hurt or the threat to our self-will. Any real love worthy of the name is a danger to our self-love. Much that passes for love of another is actually love of self in subtle disguise. The history of romantic love* has numerous examples of how men and women have tried to escape these threats by false and spurious synthetic forms of love. The classic example of romantic love which has served as an archetype for all others is the myth of Tristram and Iseult. It is a very ancient story with several versions, but the broad outline is this: Tristram is adopted by his un-

* There are a number of studies of romantic love. Among the best are: Denis de Rougement, *Love in the Western World* (Doubleday, Anchor Book); and C. S. Lewis, *Allegory of Love* (Oxford, Galaxy Book).

cle King Mark and subsequently sent on a mission to fetch Iseult, who is to be King Mark's Queen. By mistake, Tristram and Iseult drink a love potion on board ship which causes them to fall helplessly and inextricably in love with each other. Thus, the scene is set for the conditions of romantic love. Tristram cannot marry Iseult because she is to be his stepfather's wife. Also, on becoming the Queen, she will be placed, so to speak, on the royal pedestal in full view of the court. This separated nearness will provide the romantic agony, the exquisite anguish. These, then, are the ingredients of classical romantic love in western literature. Agony and anguish—the food of self-pity—exist in the attenuated, impossible situation. It becomes a love based upon man's desire to fulfill himself on his own terms. Another important element is that the major figures in these tragedies obviously do not really know each other. They are convenient objects upon which each projects his self-love. There is an unmistakable narcissism, or self-love, in which the partner is not loved for what she or he really is but as the means for fulfillment of the other's desire. Each is only an idealized symbol. When Tristram is separated from Iseult for some time, he finds another Iseult, this time Iseult of the White Hand rather than Iseult the Fair. He must have some convenient object to place on a pedestal which will personify the gratification of his own narcissistic needs. It does not matter who the person is as long as the elements of romanticism are present.

There is a real danger in this false love system. It works only as long as the partners are separated. The danger is marriage; marriage with its intimate and naked confrontation reveals the hollow bankruptcy of this nonsense. As long as any Tristram and Iseult are separated, their "love" can be credible. They can be so fed with self-pity, so contorted in tragic agony and so racked in exquisite anguish, that the emptiness of their self-love is undiscovered and unseen. In marriage each would discover a quite different person from the one projected in his romantic dream, and there would follow the mutual and natural resentment of being loved not for one's own sake but only for that of some ideal. Even more shocking would be the necessity of, and threat in, living so closely with another person's self-love. It is no wonder that marriage looms as a great threat to this romantic love, for it reveals the emptiness and self-centeredness in this elaborate dodge of romanticism.

It is interesting in this light to note the Platonic element in romantic love. The Platonic, or ideal, love seeks to avoid what it sees as the spiritually dangerous communication of the flesh. Almost without exception the partners in it have no relationship but the most Platonic. A slip occurs here or there, but never, even outside marriage, is there a significant and intimate relationship because, as a marriage, this too might carry a threat. In such an intimate relationship the two lovers would actually have a chance to meet each other and not merely dream of each other or the ideal. This, too, might expose the myth and the real inadequacy of the so-called love affair. Where do we find an example of married love glorified in our literature of romance? It must be impossible, illicit, or both, to provide the anguish which feeds self-pity and self-love. Who are the representatives of romantic love in our literature? They are Lancelot and King Arthur's wife Guinevere, Romeo and Juliet who hardly know each other, Laura whom Petrarch sees once as a young girl, and Beatrice with whom Dante is only slightly better acquainted. These are the so-called love affairs in our romantic tradition. Isn't it conveniently safe from the threat of real love to love someone you once saw a decade ago and with whom there is but small hope of any actual encounter that might dispel the fantasy of ideals?

A song in the forties, entitled "Laura," seemed to be more than a coincidental echo of Petrarch's fourteenth-century praise of Laura. The words of the song expressed the ideal of a projected image carrying no threat of real encounter. Laura is "the face in the train that is passing through . . ." She is the "face in the misty night." She is not the face across the breakfast table or the face with tears running down her cheeks over the death of your child, making demands on one's heart and life, and threatening the isolated, if lonely, comfort of self-love. In fact, Laura is not even real flesh and blood, "for she's only a dream." Dreams are really safe because they don't come true.

The terrible result of this seductive dream of romantic love is that it feeds self-pity, safeguards self-love, and detains us from realizing its ultimate emptiness. As long as we can dream of the girl in the passing train, or of a neighbor's husband who represents the unattainable and impossible fulfillment of our needs, we do not have to face the self-destructiveness of those needs. As long as we can avoid real love, we can still believe in this lie of exquisitely tragic impossible romance. The actual tragedy, however, lies in the fact that this lie can only be upheld by the unattainable quality of the fantasy. As soon as there is any real confrontation the lie becomes obvious, and the need for a different kind of love is made quickly apparent. In our fear we can successfully avoid real love by having a never-ending succession of dreams that turn out to be people. In our narcissistic lust we move from dream to dream, only to make the same uncomfortable discovery, that living closely with this new person also exposes our emptiness. Then the process begins again, relationship or marriage is regarded as "a mistake," while our true desires are once again whoring after safer dreams of unattainable faces in "the misty night."

The classical form of the romantic story usually drags out the experience, adding ever-increasing dimensions of anguish at this separated nearness. It carefully avoids any real togetherness of lovers and is only resolved in death. Death is indeed the only resolution of the self-pity of romantic tragedy. Tristram and Iseult, and Romeo and Juliet have in death the only answer to the ever-increasing anguish. In modern times there is a new death to end romantic love, the "death" of marriage. "The Anniversary Waltz" can only commend the life of romantic love up to and including the wedding night. "Oh, how we danced on the night we were wed . . ." This seems to be the most that can be commended, but it is a false and misleading lie, one nurtured by self-pity and based on the fear to love.

Professor Harvey Cox has pointed out* that one magazine for men, with a readership that easily exceeds all serious political, cultural, and religious magazines put together, is based very clearly upon a philosophy which approves the escape from love. Ostensibly it is a "girly" magazine with a heavy emphasis upon sex, but underneath, it subtly exploits the notion that all things (including women) are gadgets or toys for the male reader. He does not have to become involved (the only real "sin") because girls are only leisure-time accessories (the ideal type never makes any demands) and the reader can have his dream and his isolated independence, too. Professor Cox points out that the fault of the magazine is not that it is sexual, but that it is ultimately anti-sexual.

* In *Christianity and Crisis,* XXI:6, April 17, 1961.

This tradition of romantic love probably had its origin in the eleventh-century Albigensian protest against the medieval church. This heretical group accused the Roman Church of turning the Gospel backwards. Christianity they saw was a religion of love, *amor*, which the Church of Rome had inverted, *Roma*. All heresies have some truth in them, but this became an exceedingly misleading one, encouraging man to believe that the real source of his difficulty and sin was his body. The ideal life, in the context of Albigensian thought, is one lived as little as possible in the flesh. Our tradition of romantic love, following many of these assumptions, continues to lead us to live our lives on the basis of hiding from our real problem and its solution.

Let us see what happens in a contemporary instance of this romantic outlook. John and Jane invited Bill and Mary several months ago to a cook-out in the back yard. Bill went inside to help Jane get ice from the refrigerator. As they were getting the tray unstuck, their hands touched . . . and one thing led to another until they are "hopelessly in love." Jane's life now takes on the dimension of romance. Jane feels she is in that long tradition of Iseult, Juliet, and Rita Hayworth. Each couple has children, and so they are caught in an impossible situation. Her feelings are not unlike those of her own children when they pout. There is a delicious sadness with which she can curl up in a corner, feeling sorry for herself. She now has an excuse for everything, "If only I could be married to Bill!" She has been seduced not as much by Bill as by her own *eros,* her own desire to fulfill herself on her own terms. This love which needs to be radically transformed in the demands of marriage resists this change by dreams of "romance." The inclination toward this romanticism is caused much more by the desire to escape from realizing the inadequacy of one's own self-love than from the external attractions. As long as she only dreams, Jane does not have to face the demands of actually living with Bill; and she can explain any inadequacy in her relationship with John on the grounds that he is not Bill. All this can be, and is a thousand times over, an elaborate screen that hides us from that love which we so desperately need.

We need a love that suffers long, is kind, envies not, does not vaunt itself, is not puffed up, does not behave unseemly, seeks not its own, is not easily provoked, thinks no evil, rejoices not in iniquity, but rejoices in the truth, bears all things, endures all things, a love that never fails. (I Cor. 13) This love we need in our hearts, families, business, country, and world. It is called *agape* in contrast to the *eros* that seeks to fulfill itself on its own terms. This *eros* shows itself in every area of life in which we try to implement our wills, in sex, business, politics, or society. Our fear of *agape* reflects our unwillingness to have our willful *eros* changed.

Fear seeks to meet the threat of love in some form of isolation, and the tension in the cult of romantic love is finally resolved only in death. Here is the way, in our hiding from God and his love, we point our lives toward isolation and death. One of the characteristics of damnation is final, lonely isolation. Hell is not where God consigns unwilling persons, but hell is the desired fruit of man's unaltered will. In our fear we desire separation and thus point our lives to the ultimate isolation of hell. But it is from hell and death that the Gospel sets us free.

How does our worship allow God's love to overcome our fear and free us from isolation and death? First, the Christian Gospel does not tell us that our natural desires are in themselves evil. We do not have to eradicate our self-will and self-love. There is something good about our needs and their fulfillment. We are not taught that God will love us to the extent that we hate ourselves. All romantic love has something within it that is good and something for which to be grateful. The drive that sends us out of ourselves, even if distorted and ultimately empty of real love, has an embryonic goodness about it. In a simple sentence John Donne describes how God deals with our self-love. "Grace never destroys nature." Nature is a yet unfinished creation and needs re-creating. Grace redeems, transforms, and fulfills nature. God's love does not destroy our love but builds upon it and fulfills it.

This fact is nowhere better illustrated than in Dante's *Divine Comedy*. In many inescapable ways Beatrice is an outstanding example of the tragic distortion of love that began in the Middle Ages. Although Beatrice was an historical personage known to Dante in Florence, there is great debate among scholars as to exactly what she represents. One thing, however, is very clear. She is not his wife. While Dante is exiled he mourns for everything about his beloved city of Florence, but he does not so much as mention his wife. Beatrice, whom he never really knew well (and is thus a convenient object of romantic love), is the figure who leads Dante into Paradise where even Virgil cannot go. Now the glorious thing about Christianity, which Dante did understand, is shown as Beatrice leads the love she has evoked from Dante past herself toward God. Despite the inadequate and unfortunate quality of Dante's love for Beatrice it is used to bring him out of himself, from behind his fears, to God.* Few people have understood better than Dante this wonderful theme of Christian love, that God can take our self-love, with all its

* Cf. Charles Williams, *The Figure of Beatrice.*

distortion, inadequacy, and ultimate self-destructive quality, and use it gracefully without destroying it.

It is impossible to exaggerate what a wonderful action this is. God can build upon and redeem even the worst situations. A marriage begun with only the emptiest selfish motives can become the occasion of unknowable love and joy. The unfortunate motives that led one into business or the ministry or marriage can be built upon, changed, and transformed. In fact, they can be looked upon in deep gratitude for bringing one to the place where he can be changed. Who has had an even slightly successful marriage and does not look back with gratitude to the selfish need that brought him to marriage? The desire to make money, to seek power, to be needed, and to gain fame are expressions of man's self-love. Technical theological terms such as "concupiscence" and *eros* have been used to describe this self-based power in man. However, the point that needs noting is that the natural drives of man need not be destroyed or eradicated; they need to be changed, transformed, and rededicated. Dante understood that the sins of drive and power, of life and love, were ultimately less serious than the internal sins of anger, envy, and pride. Christianity has frequently, and incorrectly, been represented as demanding the eradication of nature and the destruction of the powers of self. On the contrary, our Lord reminds us that he came that we might have life and have it more abundantly, that all these things he has told us that we might have joy, and that our joy might be full.

As Dante saw his love for Beatrice, turned and transformed by the love of God, so all Christians in worship are given the opportunity to have their self-based desires and drives turned and redeemed. For this to occur in worship we must first realize how these drives of self-love by themselves are the sources of self-injury or separation from our neighbor and from God, leading us ultimately to death. The specific occasions of these facts are expressed in confession. Because we love ourselves first and wish the world conformed to our wills, we have been thoughtless and cruel, we have violated the rights and wills of others, and we have rebelled against God's will. These matters include everything from the letters we have not written, the hurt we have caused others, to the failure even to acknowledge our rebellion against God. Then, in the offertory in Holy Communion we present the symbols of these God-given but humanly-distorted powers. The bread and wine offered represent both God's creation and our power over it. The grain that is grown is harvested, processed, and baked before being presented. The wine is grown and carefully fermented. Here we have representations of God's creation and our stewardship over it, of our wills and skills, and of our powers and drives. The money that we offer is an expression of our talents and services. It becomes a link with the entire life of the Church. Our presented alms help remind us of our connection and part in the mission field, urban evangelism, institutional service, and the prophetic criticism of social injustice. Our prayers express our anxieties, cares, and concerns. In these four, bread, wine, money, and prayers, we begin the redirection of our self-based love. In confession and absolution another opportunity is given for the transformation of our wills and drives, and the offering of "our selves, our souls and bodies," is the culmination of our confession, offering, oblation, and sacrifice.

All this is the ground work for that which overcomes our fear to love. The climax of our worship is found in communion, in meeting and receiving the very love of God, which overcomes fear and nurtures our ability to love in this new and abundant way. Two things are essential to remember in connection with communion: our *empty hands* and our *thanksgiving*. That great Hastings hymn well expresses the bit about our hands. "In my hands no price I bring, simply to thy cross I cling." This is a communion with empty hands, hands which carry only the wrinkles and calluses of their history, a history of being instruments of our wills. Our hands are deeply personal. They have helped and they have hurt. The same hand that has placed a bill on the alms basin is perhaps the hand that has slapped a child's face in impatience or anger. Hands count money, bend beer cans, write checks, make biscuits, become fists, point fingers, remove cancers, dig ditches, shoot guns, and deliver babies. One of the last utterances of our Lord hanging on the cross was "into thy hands I commend my spirit." Hands are instruments of wills as nothing else seems to be. Therefore, they have an unusual symbolic power in standing for the expressions of all man's longing, need, desire, ambition, self-assertiveness, concupiscence, *eros,* and willfulness. The tragedy of man is that these things are at the same time both his grandeur and his malady. The great Evangel shows us that they do not need to be destroyed but redeemed. In fact these even become the instruments by which we receive that love which transforms them. It is into the calloused, empty instruments of our guilt and shame, our inadequacy and self-sabotage, that the bread of life is placed. As Dante seemed to understand, his love for Beatrice, with all its subtle selfishness and ultimate inadequacy, started his moving out of the hermit's cave of safe isolation. So it is with our drives, no matter how selfish and inadequate they initially are. They at least begin to pull us out of fear into the tragedy of life where it becomes increasingly clear how desperately we need that which is nothing less than the love of God. "Our hearts are restless and will always be until they find their rest in thee," is a profound statement about both life and worship. All our desires are a symptom of our need for God. At that moment in the service of Holy Communion as we put forth our empty hands, we are presenting the instruments of our will to be that upon which is placed the instrument of God's love, his body.

In addition to hands we need to remember thanksgiving. The unique quality of gratitude in all our love is given by God's grace. The deepest quality of Christian charity is thanksgiving. There is no self-pity in gratitude. It is opposed to envy, self-seeking, resentment, acquisitiveness, and bitterness, the milestones along the way to death. The prayer for trustfulness begins with the theme of gratitude.

O most loving Father, who willest us to give thanks for all things, to dread nothing but the loss of thee, and to cast all our care on thee, who carest for us; Preserve us from faithless fears and worldly anxieties, and grant that no clouds of this mortal life may hide from us the light of that love which is immortal, and which thou has manifested unto us in thy Son, Jesus Christ our Lord.

Too often this initial basis of gratitude is passed over too lightly. Does it really mean that we are to give thanks for all things, for pain and suffering, tragedy and death? God can take whatever we offer in worship and make it graceful in ways it could not have been before.

It is relatively easy to give thanks for good things like food, health, children, safety, and peace. But it is much more difficult to give thanks "for all things," for a toothache, hunger, death, or the silent tragedies about which we do not speak.

130

A young mother once endured a most horrible tragedy that she did not feel she could share with anyone but her doctor, her cook, and her minister. The hurt was too deep for tears and one she would never desire anyone she loved to experience. Yet some time after it was all over, she told her minister, "I'm not sure you'll understand this, but I'm not sorry it happened." In one sense, of course, she was terribly sorry and deeply penitent. But, on another level, she had learned something of God's love and power she had never before known, and her whole life had a new dimension. Because this tragedy was taken up in a life of worship, the hurt was allowed to tear away the fear and self-sufficiency which, as clouds of this mortal life, had separated her from the love of God. Because we have cast all our care on him who carest for us, we need dread nothing but the loss of God; and we, therefore, can give thanks for all things.

CHAPTER EIGHT

Worship and Eternal Life

THE KNOWLEDGE of death is more a part of us than we are apt to realize. All our other fears are overshadowed and permeated by this deeper and final fear, the fear to die. However, it is so great that we are frequently unaware of its power over us, and we strongly resist acknowledging our ultimate end. It has always been so, this difficulty of facing death, but it is much more apparent in our times than in almost any other period of history.

We feel quite superior to the nineteenth century with its relative taboo about sex and claim much courage in our "frank" and "daring" treatment of this subject in movies, novels, drama, and instruction in schools. However, the twentieth century has what amounts to a cowardly conspiracy of silence regarding a taboo all its own, death, the inevitable end of us all. One of the marked contrasts in the literature of the two centuries is how rarely present-day literature deals with a death scene. It is perfectly astonishing that a number of otherwise good books dealing with man's fears fail to deal with or mention the fear of death. *Memento mori,* "remember death," was a not uncommon greeting and practical admonition in the Middle Ages when death was prepared for in this life. This greeting today would sound more like a cry of despair. The very fact of death is elaborately avoided. Even in learned magazines appear advertisements for rust-proof and water-proof caskets made by "experts in the use of space-age materials." Today's funeral customs of the irreligious are as superstitious and incongruous as at almost any time in history—a fact which did not escape Evelyn Waugh and furnished him with the material for his bitingly satirical book *The Loved One.*

Contemporary man's ability to avoid facing such a rational and demonstrable fact as death is absolutely incredible. One popular and growing religious body in this country simply denies the fact of death and has persisted in doing so for generations in the face of what can be only the most obvious evidence to the contrary. It is not at all unusual in conferences for groups discussing their fears to list everything from termites to H-bombs but to fail to list death. This is certainly not so because the fear is insignificant, but rather because it is so great we would hide from even recognizing it.

One reason for our culture's timidity in regard to the subject of death is the unusual pretension of the twentieth century to self-sufficiency. Every individual in every age is tainted with a desire to be independent of God. Today, however, we have produced a degree of independence never before attained. Never have we been so tempted, at least externally, to do without God. Some claim actually to foresee a time when mankind will have successfully overcome war, pestilence, and famine. The question remains, however, what do we do about death—now? To be told that death is overcome by the historical continuance of corporate mankind is of little help to the individual facing his ineluctable end. In spite of science, progress, medicine, and even spiritual healing the mortality rate is still 100 per cent. No wonder we seek to avoid the thought of death! It is an embarrassing and awkward difficulty in any scheme of human self-sufficiency.

Characteristics of the culture affect the Christian, too. We cannot live and breathe in this climate without partaking of its feeling. The Christian Church, because of its involvement in the twentieth-century world, has many of the same limitations as the culture. Edna St. Vincent Millay expresses the malady of our times in her poem *Conversation at Midnight*. The figure Ricardo says:

Man has never been the same since God died,
He has taken it very hard.

Why, you'd think it was only yesterday,
The way he takes it.

Not that he says much, but he laughs much louder than he
used to.
And he can't bear to be left alone even for a moment.
And he can't sit still . . .

He gets along pretty well as long as it's daylight:
He works very hard,
And he amuses himself very hard with the many cunning
amusements
This clever age affords.
But it's no use; the moment it begins to get dark,
As soon as it's night
He goes out and howls over the grave of God.

We can scarcely avoid being affected by this atmosphere of our culture. Even the resurgence of interest in religion in the forties and the growth of the churches after World War II was and is characterized in the main by self-help religion or by simply concern for this world. The world view of the age, assuming as it does, that God is dead, leads men to construct their endeavors apart from God and causes even Christians to avoid the reality of death. We have been led to concentrate our Christianity upon hygienic psychology, morals, and the things of this world. Therefore, any one of us can safely assume that he has been partially deprived of the full power of faith because of the common cultural failure to face the reality of 'death. Accordingly, we must examine our fear of death in all its manifestations and aspects, in spite of our natural and cultural reluctance to do so, in order that we may see how God's love overcomes our fear to die.

Why do we fear death? The most obvious reason is that it is the greatest and final change. Loss of the familiar and entry into the unknown frequently causes anxiety. The test of change caused by bereavement is one of the most merciless faith undergoes. The death of a friend or a member of our family forces us to reorder our loyalties. This process is never easy. We must gradually face the little everyday necessities which are different now that our child, for example, is dead. Simple things must be changed. What shall we do with his toys or clothes? Moreover, we must change the way we are living and our expectations of the future. At first we are startled to realize one day, when the time comes around to bring him home from nursery school, that he needs never to be brought home from school again. In these periods it takes time, indeed, to rearrange our lives and face the agony of change.

Fear of death is behind all fear of change. Going from one culture to another has been found to put people in emotionally precarious situations. The change from things familiar to strange, in language, dress, customs, ideas, and looks, places real stress upon people and often causes great distress. The Armed Forces, State Department, and missionary societies have found that people crossing cultural frontiers are subject to this "culture shock." In the new situation the person often becomes depressed, short-tempered, and subject to temptations which heretofore did not apply. On the other hand, those individuals able to adapt effectively, without succumbing to "culture shock," seem to be the exception. In attempting to distinguish the abilities of men and to learn the causes of culture shock, both the churches and government have begun to examine some of the deepest levels of the human spirit. Actually, it is a remarkable fact that some of the most creative and exciting theology is being produced in the mission field. Men who have survived the experience of change and the shock of newness are able to look back upon "home" with a freshness and perception which they did not have before.

The significance of this fact is that not to change is not to grow, and not to grow is to die. The mature and growing person is able to make the change. Whoever is afraid of change is afraid to grow and afraid to live. Those who fear it surround themselves with the things that are "theirs," clinging desperately to them against the inevitable tugs of time, much the way a child clings to the dirty blanket that has comforted him since the cradle. Rabindranath Tagore has expressed this relationship between change and growth thus:

There are people who have a static concept of life and thus only long for a life after death since they are interested exclusively in continuance but not in fulfillment; they are happy in the illusion that the things to which they got used will last forever. In their thought, they identify themselves fully with their usual environment and with all that they have collected. The necessity of leaving them all means death to them. They forget that the true meaning of life is to live beyond, the constant growing beyond oneself. The fruit sticks to the stem, the shell to the flesh, the flesh to the stone as long as the fruit is not ripe, as long as this is, it is not ready for further life development.*

In addition to change, guilt is usually another uncomfortable concomitant of death. Should we stop now to reflect how we would feel if someone very close to us were suddenly to die, we would most likely discover that a nagging element of our sorrow is that we failed to do something for him which we had intended doing. This is especially true when we confront the death of one of our parents. Death cuts us off from the possibility of telling them how grateful we are or how much we love them, and our recent failure to write or visit them can never be rectified. Indeed, death rings the bell on all procrastination. All intentions are now too late. Death makes us guilty for our lack of love. Thus every death is a reminder of our death. Measles or cancer does not have the threat of universality but death is something we must all face. This is seen in that oft quoted observation of John Donne about the tolling of the funeral bell, "Send not to ask for whom the bell tolls. It tolls for thee." No man is an island, and each death is a reminder of our own. Both in the death of others and in our own our chances are ended to make amends, and all our procrastinating dreams die, too.

Another reason we fear death is that judgment is involved. The strong calm confidence in the face of an imminent con-

* Quoted by Hans Hofmann in *Official Register of Harvard University,* LV:23, April 25, 1958.

frontation with God is perhaps the luxury of only the arrogantly self-deluded. On the other hand, because of his spiritual insight, the saint is perhaps more aware than anyone of the sinful discrepancy between what he is and what God has required of him. Hence, he is neither casual nor cocky at the prospect of meeting his Maker. Every honest and humble man must have some real trepidation of this encounter. This stems from no fear of brimstone and fire. Instead, it need only be a limited understanding of the quality of God's love before which our life can be hardly more than sadly empty.

G. A. Studdert-Kennedy has captured something of the pain in the judgment of love in his poem, "Well?" about a soldier in World War I who was repelled by the dismal, crude pictures of judgment day painted by his chaplain until he had a dream which, though a dream, was more real than most waking experiences. He dreamed that he had died and was confronting, face to face, Almighty God. Looking into God's indescribable eyes, he sees his whole life, all the mean things he had done, the things he should have done, the person he had not become. Then he begins to feel a poignant and excruciating sadness about his life, seen thus through the eyes of God.

> And then at last 'E said one word,
> 'E just said one word—"Well?"
> And I said in a funny voice,
> "Please can I go to 'Ell?"
> And 'E stood there and looked at me,
> And 'E kind o' seemed to grow,
> Till 'E shone like the sun above my 'ead,
> And then 'E answered "No,
> You can't that 'Ell is for the blind,
> And not for those that see.
> You know that you 'ave earned it, lad,

So you must follow Me.
Follow Me on by the paths o' pain,
Seeking what you 'ave seen,
Until at last you can build the 'Is'
Wi' the brick o' the 'Might have been.' "
That's what 'E said, as I'm alive,
And that there dream were true.
But what 'E meant—I don't quite know,
Thou' I knows what I 'as to do.
I's got to follow that I's seen,
Till this old carcass dies;
For I daren't face in the land of grace
The sorrow o' those eyes.
There ain't no throne, and there ain't no books,
It's 'Im you've got to see,
It's 'Im, just 'Im, that is the Judge
Of blokes like you and me.
And, boys, I'd sooner frizzle up,
I' the flames of a burnin' 'Ell
Than stand and look into 'Is face
And 'ear 'Is voice say—"Well?" *

Sometimes we can fool ourselves that we do not really fear death, because we believe we are ready to die. This readiness, however, may simply be a mere weary resignation to the biological process. Some readiness to die can be more like spiritual suicide and defeat than a holy Christian victory. No, resignation is not the answer to our fears. We overcome this fear of death by love through worship. Our victory lies in our baptized death. Just as every fear is overshadowed and permeated by fear of death, so the solution to each fear, on the very deepest level, is an overcoming of the fear of death. The man who successfully leaves his familiar surroundings and functions well in new ones obviously has a fi-

* G. A. Studdert-Kennedy, "Well?" in *The Best of G. A. Studdert-Kennedy,* (New York: Harper & Bros., 1948), p. 164.

delity to, and dependence upon, something higher than his possessions or environment. We fear death because it is the last frontier, the final test of our loyalties and fidelities. If we have truly "loved God for God's sake," then we can cross this frontier in the same spirit we leave any earthly home to go to another. The entire life of worship is one in which we learn and grow in life, while yet in the midst of death.

We have seen that we are afraid to be honest, to care, to be humble, to fail, to be human, and to love. As each of these fears is met in the whole life of worship, not merely in particular services, the fear of death is overcome. Each of these fears represents the necessity to let go at certain stages of growth. We need to give up our self-delusions and lies, and to live in God's real world. We need to give up our destructive defenses against hurt in our fear to care and have our hearts opened to God's love. We need to let our pride be changed into that humble and grateful spirit we see in Christ himself. We need to release our fear of failure by having it burned clean in the tortuous judgment of the Crucifixion and by giving up ourselves to God's service which transcends all other loyalties and loves. We need to give up the temptations which leave us dead inside, and to be made into that perfect humanity which we behold in the humble Lord. And we need to offer our self-will, self-love, and self-dependence to be redeemed by the self-giving love of God.

The theme throughout these chapters has been the scriptural one of the drama of life and death. "The wages of sin is death but the gift of God is eternal life." The wages of fear and separation, of dishonesty and imperviousness, of spiritual arrogance and cowardice, yes, of love itself, is the death of eternity begun now. The love of God that casts out and overcomes this fear through the life of worship brings the quality of eternal life now. Yet how is it, some may ask, that the answer to this final fear of death and all its threats is itself a type of death? How can we distinguish the death to self which is living our baptism, loving God for his sake, and walking the way of the Cross from the death of suicide, isolation, "zombiehood," fear and sin? There is no more difficult question in life than the choices between these two deaths. One is the dreadful terminus of nothing and the other is the wrenching transition to new and final dimensions of fullness, glory, love, and life. Neither begins with the biological death of this body. Both are participated in, and begun, here on earth.

How do we know? How do we know that death is this great wondrous portal to final change? The only way to know is through the knowledge of faith. Faith is our response to God's love through the life of worship. Now is the time to begin. We only know of God's love beyond death by the faith that grows in the confessing, forgiven, honest, human offering of self in this life to our God. We know now something of why the psalmist bids us: "O worship the Lord in the beauty of holiness; let the whole earth stand in awe of him."

No spiritual "Dr. Spock book" can give us the guidance we need. Some good things can be used for evil ends. Some bad things and experiences can be the occasion of creative love and redemption. The only bridge between death and life is worship. Only in the life of worship can the good things be truly and ultimately good and the bad things be redeemed by their being offered to God to be forgiven, redeemed and sanctified.

Fear of death is indistinguishable from any other fear because all fears are ultimately tied up with this one. Honesty, caring, humility, humanity, and love cannot possibly be separated from life itself. All are integral parts of the Christian's worship. Worship is the life of Good Friday and Easter. The probing pain of the Law, the agonizing honesty in facing responsibility and guilt, the hurts that come to pride, each experience of failure, the desires to withdraw from full participation in the vulnerability of life, the fear of wrenched wills, broken hearts, transformed love, and nothingness, are buried with Christ, who overcomes death. Each new awareness of this Gospel, every forgiven sin, each grateful power of life, and all warm human loves are reborn and fortified in our newly risen creation of Easter. "For God hath not given us the spirit of fear but of love and power and a sound mind."

At the Lord's Table, the foretaste of the age to come, our whole life of worship is dramatized. The themes of honesty driving out self-pity, forgiveness taking us back and empowering us to care, are over-shadowed by the flood of compassion that flows from the broken dam of our arrogance. In the background is the ever-recurring strain of penitential unworthiness overcome by God's forgiveness. Then, as with a crash of cymbals, the sight of our humble Lord, showing us who we really are, draws out of our hearts the poison of bitterness and the fear of being human. This symphony is not without its painful dissonances of judgment as we see who we are and the hurt we have caused God's love. And yet, at the same time, blended but distinguishable are the powerful strains of resolution coming from the healed consciences of cowards to stand and speak within the Christian society for the kingdom of God, cost what it will. The themes of offering, confession, oblation, and dedication mount to a crescendo in the fulfilling sacrifice of empty-handed response to that sacrifice of Christ. In partaking of this ultimate banquet the final victory and completion of God's will is celebrated. The finale which completes the rhythm responds in praise and thanksgiving and in the calm, quiet blessing of peace. This is no mere service. It is a *whole and eternal life.*

SUGGESTED QUESTIONS FOR GROUP DISCUSSION

This book is about our common malady, fear. "We are afraid to be honest, to care, to be humble, to fail, to be human, and to love. . . . [and] we fear death. . . . The love of God . . . casts out and overcomes this fear through the life of worship."

Having read *Fear, Love, and Worship,* members of a parish group, with a leader, can develop a series of discussions around questions like these:

Chapter 1: *Worship.* "All times and all places can be occasions of worship. . . . Every house is God's house." (p. 20) What kinds of experience can, in the widest sense, be called the "worship" that brings God's presence into the lives of people like us who are members of this parish?

Chapter 4: *The Fear of Being Humble.* How would **Jean** Baptiste, in Albert Camus' *The Fall* (pp. 72ff.), have behaved differently if he had possessed the spiritual endowments of the Cardinal in *The Prisoner* (pp. 64ff.)? Explain *why* his behavior would have been different.

Chapter 5: *The Fear of Failure.* Do you live in a community that is "possessed by fear" of failure? (p. 87) If this is so (or if you know of a community where this situation exists), can this fear be healed as Lucius Cary's could be healed? (pp. 97-100) *How,* by the ministry of the laity, would this healing take place in the community?

Chapter 6: *The Fear of Being Human.* If a man like Jimmy Porter in *Look Back in Anger* is "afraid to be human" because he fears freedom, responsibility, and guilt (p. 104), how would you explain to him that this fear could be relieved by the Holy Communion? And how would Jimmy Porter's fear be relieved if he could develop a disposition like that of the boy who gave blood for a transfusion? (p. 115)

Chapter 8: *Worship and Eternal Life.* What has happened, in this discussion group, that can help us to "overcome this fear of death by love through worship?" (p. 139)

[NOTE: The foregoing page references are to this text.]